E. B. WHITE

on

DOGS

Katharine S. White, E. B. White, and Minnie in Maine

E. B. WHITE
on
DOGS

Edited by Martha White

TILBURY HOUSE PUBLISHERS
Gardiner, Maine

Tilbury House, Publishers
103 Brunswick Avenue
Gardiner, Maine 04345
800-582-1899 • www.tilburyhouse.com

First edition: May 2013
10 9 8 7 6 5 4 3 2 1

Cataloging-in-Publication Data
White, E. B. (Elwyn Brooks), 1899-1985.
[Works. Selections]
E. B. White on dogs / edited by Martha White. -- First hardcover edition.
    pages cm
ISBN 978-0-88448-341-0 (hardcover : alk. paper) -- ISBN 978-0-88448-342-7 (pbk. : alk. paper)
1. White, E. B. (Elwyn Brooks), 1899-1985 Knowledge--Dogs. 2. Dogs--Literary collections. 3. Human-animal relationships--Literary collections. I. White, Martha, 1954 Dec. 18 - II. Title.
PS3545.H5187A6 2013
818'.5209--dc23
                                    2012048622

All photographs are courtesy of the E. B. White Estate, unless otherwise noted.
Jacket front: E. B. White and Minnie, North Brooklin, Maine.
Jacket back: Minnie being interviewed in E. B. White's New York office.
Copyediting (as allowed . . .): Genie Dailey, Fine Points Editorial Services, Jefferson, Maine.
Photo scanning by Christine Olmstead, Before & After Photo, Brunswick, Maine.
Printed and bound by the Maple Press, York, Pennsylvania.

For my husband, Taylor Allen,
with all my love

"You have to watch out about dachshunds—some of them are as delicately balanced as a watch. . . ."

Contents

EBW and his granddaughter, Martha White

Introduction: "A Chronic Perplexity"

When E. B. White wrote an obituary for a Scotty dog, "an opinionated little bitch," and published it in *The New Yorker* in early 1932, few readers blinked an eye. They were accustomed to reading about Daisy, her likes (the iceman) and dislikes (doormen and horses), and her run-ins with the law. They already knew that her vet wore spats and called her "Whitie" (she was jet black), they had felt her humiliation when she was kicked out of Schrafft's, and they had sympathized when she was arrested. After Daisy was run down by a Yellow Cab that had jumped the curb, White's "Obituary" added his diagnosis of her "curious habit of holding people firmly by the ankle without actually biting them—a habit that gave her an immense personal advantage and won her many enemies." As he understood it, "she suffered from a chronic perplexity, and it relieved her to take hold of something."

My grandfather also suffered from a chronic perplexity, I believe, and he spent his career trying to take hold of it, not infrequently through the literary device of his dogs. Daisy had been the sole attendant at my grandparents' wedding in 1929. "It was a very nice wedding—nobody threw anything, and there was a dog fight," my grandfather later recalled. It was natural, then, that the same Scotty dog spoke for him, through a letter to his wife, when White wanted to tell her how happy he was that she was pregnant with his first child. He had "been stewing around for two days now" but was so "beside himself," and "hoppy" that Daisy had decided to write to Katharine on his behalf.

Between E. B. White's birth in Mount Vernon, New York, on July 11, 1899, and his own obituary in October 1985, he owned over a dozen dogs of various breeds—collies, setters, lab retrievers, Scotties, terriers, dachshunds, and mongrel mixes. I was personally familiar with about half of them and I read about the others. Some appeared in his *New Yorker* "Talk of the Town" entries; Daisy and Fred (and also a goose) were interviewed on serious subjects of the day including space travel and Watergate; and many different breeds appeared in poems and sketches and even on the occasional Christmas card. In the early days of White's comments for *The New Yorker*, the city dog shows were an annual topic for amusement and observations on changing styles and trends. In his "Turtle Bay Diary," White wrote, "The Dog Show is the only place I know of where you can watch a lady go down on her knees in public to show off the good points of a dog, thus obliterating her own."

Fred's "fraudulent reports" from the country kept appearing long after that dachshund had died on New Year's Eve, 1948 "of his excesses and after a drink of brandy." He had been "possessed of the vital spark" for just thirteen years and four months, but his spark had a habit of rekindling whenever White was puzzling out some new perplexity. Fred's "dissenting nature" and "corrosive grin" were brought to bear on Truman and Stevenson and Khruschev, and you can imagine that he had a lot to say, almost a decade posthumously, about the Russians sending a dog into space. Fred was the "dishonorable pallbearer staggering along in the rear" in the essay "Death of a Pig," an "ignoble old vigilante" with a "quest for truth." My grandfather often had to remind himself, "He was also a plain damned nuisance."

Like my grandfather, Fred was "a window gazer and a bird-watcher," peering from his vantage point on a high canopy bed on the second floor of the house in Maine. It was from that four-poster that Fred delivered his most memorable "fraudulent report" in the essay, "Bedfellows."

"'I just saw an eagle go by,' he would say. 'It was carrying a baby.'" My grandfather took care to explain, "This was not precisely a lie. Fred was like a child in many ways. . . ."

I suspect these various dogs, in all their eccentricities, were part of what allowed my grandfather to observe and express his own childlike wonder at the natural world around him, whether in the city ("Dog around the block, sniff . . .") or the country ("I knew that as soon as the puppy reached home and got his sea legs he would switch to the supplement du jour—a flake of well-rotted cow manure from my boot, a dead crocus bulb from the lawn, a shingle from the kindling box, a bloody feather from the execution block behind the barn. . . . I even introduced him to the tonic smell of coon"). White also puzzled over dogs farther afield: "The Russians, we understand, are planning to send a dog into outer space. The reason is plain enough: The little moon is incomplete without a dog to bay at it."

When I visited Tilbury House, Publishers, in Gardiner, Maine, to discuss this book project, it quickly became apparent that we had made a happy match. Tilbury House had taken in *One Man's Meat* some years ago, so they were already peddling "Dog Training" and "A Boston Terrier" and other essays with good results. Their publisher, Jennifer Bunting, had worked as my grandfather's Sunday Help for a couple of years, so she had gotten to know two of his dogs, and her offices in Gardiner were a welcome place for canines, as well. My own young golden retriever had come along for the ride. It was not until Jennifer took me around Tilbury House to introduce me to the rest of the team, however—which, as it turned out, included a feisty young parrot-in-residence named Zimmy, lording it over a high filing cabinet—that the deal was sealed. As soon as I heard that parrot's story, I thought, "Just wait until Fred gets wind of this."

My grandfather had kept a bird when he lived in an apartment in New York City, but it was a smaller breed, a parakeet named Baby. Baby got into *The New Yorker* a couple of times, as he had opinions that required expression, but he was not a live wire like Fred or Zimmy. On the other hand, Fred and that parrot have a *lot* in common. Like Zimmy with his four-drawer files, Fred also "had a dossier on almost every living creature." The Tilbury House files were topped with a thick towel to protect the contents therein from Zimmy's over-zealous deposits, often spurred by just such an impromptu visit as my own. Fred would have been unlocking the secret smells in that file cabinet in an instant, sneering all the while.

"I just saw a parrot," Fred might have reported. "He thinks he's an eagle."

I was warned not to extend a hand in greeting, lest the bird take it amiss. Zimmy's owner shared her office with another woman, who told me it had taken her six months to receive so much as a kind glance from the bird, at which point he climbed into her lap as if they were old mates, while she sat frozen with uncertainty about his intentions. Her own "chronic perplexity" may have commenced that day, and I suspect she is still trying to take hold of it.

Fred, too, "saw in every bird, every squirrel, every housefly, every rat, every skunk, every porcupine, a security risk and a present danger to the republic." Zimmy would have been no exception. I could almost hear Fred's outcry: "That bird talks? Don't expect me to listen."

Fred, like Zimmy, was a zealot and an unbeliever. Zimmy's owner had confided that her parrot could be a nuisance, and often acted like a two-year-old. That, too, sounded familiar.

"He's a picky eater," she explained. "I have to cook special meals for him."

Fred was muttering in my ear, "See? We are *nothing* alike." Fred was *not* a finicky eater; just the opposite, he would eat anything, the more bitter and repulsive the better. He liked to eat broken eggs off the cellar floor, facing trouble head-on and taking full advantage, curling his lips back even as he swallowed the raw yolks. He would sample the sudsy water from a pig's enema bag, given enough scope on his tether. (Fred had to be kept on a rope because he kept trying to subdue porcupines.)

Both Fred and Zimmy shared the ability to "blow things up to proportions that satisfied [their] imagination and . . . love of adventure." My grandfather had once described Fred as the Cecil B. DeMille of dogs, ever flamboyant and dramatic. Zimmy, too, seemed to exhibit a vital spark born of the same fiery explosion as Fred. The Tilbury House parrot was not kept on a rope, but he was relegated to his cage for periods of time and while in transit. Neither Fred nor Zimmy were fond of car rides. His owner confessed, however, that if Zimmy felt he had been caged for too long, he would throw a tantrum.

"What does a parrot tantrum look like?" I had to know.

"Well, he lies on his back on the floor of the cage and kicks his feet in the air," I was told. "Then he yells, 'I love you! I love you! Let me out!'"

Zimmy's owner added, a touch sadly, I thought, that he never expressed his feelings for her except during one of these tantrums. Likewise, my grandfather was spared any outward affection from Fred. Zimmy's mad protestations of love were calculated to free him from behind bars, and Fred, too, "tended to knock down, rather than build up, the master's ego." My grandmother insisted Fred was deeply devoted to his owner, as I suspect Zimmy is, as well, but my grandfather called it "the devotion of an opportunist," guessing it was really the tumult of the farm that Fred liked. I won't hazard a guess about the tumult at Tilbury House, but where there are dogs and birds and authors sharing quarters, you can be assured there is tumult.

The dogs that I knew personally all came after Fred. There

was another dachshund, black like Minnie, and named August, who used to sit upright on his hind legs almost indefinitely (not easy for a dachshund) and beg for macadamia nuts. My grandfather wrote to his wife and described this puppy as "another Fred, I would say, but without such a heavy charge of original sin." Augie, as we knew him, also perched under the baby grand piano in my grandfather's office and howled when certain notes were played. Part of our holiday tradition involved the grandchildren begging for the tunes that would elicit Augie's "singing," and then rewarding him with macadamias.

Later came Red, Maggie, Jones, and Susy, terriers all except for Maggie, who was a mongrel mix of collie and beagle. My family eventually adopted Maggie. She was sweet-tempered but boisterous as a pup, and my grandmother by that time had skin ailments that couldn't weather Maggie's habit of jumping up to express her affection.

Like my grandfather's first dog, a collie named Mac, Maggie accompanied me on my own chores, and thus came to be surrogate mother to five Peking ducklings whose mother had been run over. (Mrs. Treacher, I called that white duck. The drake was named Arthur Treacher, because he resembled the portly English actor whom I knew from the Merv Griffin TV show of the late 1960s.) Her nest had been built in the tall grass next to a guardrail, on the roadside opposite our pond. When the female duck failed to avoid a speeding car, Arthur Treacher soon followed, because he kept crossing the road in search of her.

My grandfather had been following these events with interest, led by Maggie to view the roadside nest with its original clutch of fifteen eggs. Upon Mrs. Treacher's untimely demise, he promptly delivered a broody hen from his farm down the road and we moved the nest into our old barn, candled the eggs to choose those most likely to succeed, and the hen finished the incubation. Maggie accompanied me daily to check on their progress, so it was no surprise that the ducklings imprinted on her. Once the ducklings were hardened off, we returned the borrowed hen, nearly featherless from her dedication and worry over these odd chicks who insisted on swimming. At that point, the ducklings began following the dog, all in a line and struggling to keep up, and one or two eventually learned to hitch a ride by grabbing the ruff at the back of Maggie's neck for balance, flapping their wings to gain purchase, and then riding bareback like the young circus rider standing on horseback in White's essay, "Circle of Time." Maggie was just docile enough to allow it, and she would dutifully head for the pond, where she knew they would disembark. My grandfather occasionally came over to enjoy the spectacle.

Red and Jones were alike in many ways and I mix them up, in memory; they were small, sometimes surly male terriers, each with a Napoleon complex, in my opinion. Jones "particularly distrusts women in trousers, drivers of panel trucks, small children, and stray dogs," my grandfather had written. Men in trousers were fine and women in skirts were fine, but women in trousers or the UPS man were considered an insult and a threat to the Republic. Jones would have to be banished until the threat was gone.

Susy was the final dog, a West Highland White Terrier, much-photographed for her beautiful off-white coat and pretty face. "She is as open and outgiving as Jones is closed and reserved," White wrote in 1974. "Everyone loves Susy. Everybody tries to like Jones." Black Watch Daisy's vet might have called her "Blackie," but if Susy had opinions like the Scotty bitch, they were entirely positive. The iceman would have been her friend, had there still been one. She didn't have a dissenting bone in her body, unlike Fred or Jones or Red, who rarely had an assenting one.

White had once written about a housekeeper in their employ, saying that Josephine "was the only person he knew who, when a dog got sick on the floor and she had to clean up the mess, felt sorry for the dog." In truth, though, E. B. White's sympathies were also aligned with the natural world, in all its complication, noise, and messiness. Writing about Jones (whose sire was known as Hunston Horseradish—and there was plenty of bite to Jones, as well), White said he "is seldom found more than six feet from where I am. He is a neurotic. . . . But he and I are enough alike so that we get on well, and I can't help being touched by his loyalty—which I think in his case is simply insecurity. He would never take a prize at a show. Neither would I, come to think of it."

E. B. White did take a few prizes, of course, among them a Pulitzer Prize special citation for letters in 1978, and before that, the Presidential Medal of Freedom from John F. Kennedy, presented by Maine's Senator Edmund Muskie in 1964. If he had been required to trade any of these prizes for one of his dogs, however, I suspect the dog might have won out. Asked for an interview for the *New York Times* with Israel Shenker, White commented, "I wish instead I were doing what my dog is doing at this moment, rolling in something ripe he has found on the beach in order to take on its smell. His is such an easy, simple way to increase one's stature and enlarge one's personality."

E. B. White's dogs came in every shape and style, and sometimes gave voice to the words he could not have spoken otherwise. These poems, essays, and sketches about dogs have been culled from a lifetime of his letters and comments and book collections, although interestingly, dogs did not feature largely, if at all, in White's children's books. I suspect their personalities were too dominant for the stories he chose to tell. Margalo the bird or Snowbell the cat in *Stuart Little* could take a back seat, but a dog would have needed a major role, more like Templeton's, the rat in *Charlotte's Web*.

The love that White felt for his dogs is nowhere more beautifully stated than at the end of "Dog Training" (1940). He says:

A really companionable and indispensable dog is an accident of nature. You can't get it by breeding for it, and you can't buy it with money. It just happens along. Out of the vast sea of assorted dogs that I have had dealings with, by far the noblest, the best, and the most important was the first, the one my sister sent me in a crate. He was an old-style collie, beautifully marked, with a blunt nose and great natural gentleness and intelligence. When I got him he was what I badly needed. I think probably all these other dogs of mine have been just a groping toward that old dream. I've never dared get another collie for fear the comparison would be too uncomfortable. I can still see my first dog in all the moods and mutations that memory has filed him away in, but I think of him oftenest as he used to be right after breakfast on the back porch, listlessly eating up a dish of petrified oatmeal rather than hurt my feelings. For six years he met me at the same place after school and convoyed me home—a service he thought up himself. A boy doesn't forget that sort of association.

Tilbury House has enabled me to collect these celebrations of his various dogs under one roof and offer them to E. B. White readers, new and old; I hope this book will lead you to his other work, as well. In all of his writing, which spanned nearly eight decades, White's primary declaration was much like Zimmy's "I love you, I love you!"

E. B. White gave it a few more words: "All that I hope to say in books, all that I ever hope to say, is that I love the world." When it came to a nine-to-five office job, or the trappings of celebrity, however, he and Zimmy would have been in complete agreement: "Let me out!"

A Note to the Reader

E. B. *White On Dogs* was conceived and compiled the same year that *Charlotte's Web* turned sixty and about twenty-seven years after my grandfather's death in 1985. Rereading his essay, "A Week in November" (page 78), written in 1942, however, it strikes me how little has changed and how current his words remain. His old farmhouse stands firm, well maintained and owned by another family now, but the open fields, barns, woods, and ponds look the same. There is an orchard where cattle once grazed, the big vegetable garden lies fallow, and there is no wartime egg production—but there *could* be. Fred's grave persists in the brambles, ever restless.

Meanwhile, up and down the coast, Maine farmland trusts are working to keep these old farms open for another generation of young farmers just beginning to take up their implements. Kale and chard are still improved by frost and appear in our farmer's markets, and some of the heritage varieties of tomatoes and potatoes are making a comeback. Everyone knows the word "organic," which used to be the assumption rather than the exception. Deer hunting is common and our dogs wear blaze orange vests this month; wild turkeys (and bald eagles) have made a comeback; and some of our neighbors keep pigs for slaughter.

What might be just as compelling to my grandfather is that mutts are making a comeback. Rescue dogs are in vogue, though probably not on Madison Avenue where White found Fred.

Within our own family, dogs have continued to enjoy residency, despite their various character flaws. I had three show up last Thanksgiving, besides my own young pup. Golden retrievers have replaced dachshunds as our popular breed, but there have been beagles, collies, terriers, German shepherds, and mutts, each boasting its own eccentricity. One was even named Andy, after my grandfather.

Collecting these pieces on canines, we have kept them largely as they appeared originally, not attempting to mesh the inconsistencies. The letters (each previously printed in *Letters of E. B. White*, rev. ed.) are more casual in style, and my Tilbury House editor was surprised to find that the co-author of *The Elements of Style* did not always get his *that* and *which* correct, especially in the early years. Our hands-off policy nearly killed her.

We did try to clarify identities. Elwyn Brooks White rarely was called that, but shows up as "En" and later "Andy," the latter bestowed on him at Cornell. Likewise, his wife Katharine S. (Angell) White appears as Kay or K; his sister Clara White is "Tar" Wyvell; and White has both a brother (Stan) and a friend who appear as "Bun." Fortunately, the dogs' names are easier and I have tried to note them along the way, where specific dogs were the inspiration for a piece.

Martha White

Elwyn with his mother, Jessie, and Beppo, an Irish setter;
Mount Vernon, New York

E. B. White: A Timeline

1899, July 11 Elwyn Brooks White was born to Samuel Tilly White and Jessie (Hart) White in Mount Vernon, New York, the youngest of six children: Marion, Clara, Albert, Stanley, Lillian, and Elwyn.

1913–1917 Attended Mount Vernon High School; published in the school's *Oracle*.

1917–1921 Enrolled at Cornell University; earned his nickname, Andy, after Cornell's President Andrew D. White.

1918 Registered for the draft, but was rejected for not weighing enough. Enlisted in the Student Army Training Corps at Cornell. (Armistice was declared in November.)

1920 Editor-in-Chief at the *Cornell Daily Sun*.

1921 Graduated from Cornell. Declined a teaching position and went to work (briefly) for United Press and later the American Legion News Service.

1922 Cross-country road trip with Cornell classmate Howard Cushman in White's Model T Ford, "Hotspur." Work along the way included the publication of a sonnet to a Kentucky derby horse, winning a limerick contest, selling roach powder, playing the piano, and hocking their typewriters. Took a job with the *Seattle Times*.

1923 Left for Alaska on the SS *Buford*; worked on the ship to earn his return passage. Returned to New York City and took various unsatisfying jobs in advertising, while submitting pieces to *The Conning Tower* and other publications.

1925, February 19 *The New Yorker*'s first issue; White published in the April 18, 1925, issue ("A Step Forward; The advertising man takes over the vernal account"), and next in the May 9, 1925, issue ("Defense of the Bronx River"), and others.

1926 Began part-time work for *The New Yorker*.

1927 Accepted a full-time position at *The New Yorker*.

1929 *The Lady is Cold*; and later, *Is Sex Necessary?* (co-authored with James Thurber). Married Katharine (Sergeant) Angell on November 13.

1930 Son Joel McCoun White born December 21.

1931 *Ho-Hum: Newsbreaks from The New Yorker*.

1932 *Another Ho-Hum*; April 23, E. B. White's cover for *The New Yorker*, a seahorse with an oat bag.

1933 Purchased saltwater farm in Brooklin, Maine, on Allen Cove.

1934 *Every Day Is Saturday*.

1935 Death of White's father, Samuel Tilley White.

1936 *Farewell to Model T* (with Richard Lee Strout, published under the name Lee Strout White); death of White's mother, Jessie Hart White.

1937 White's "Year of Grace" from *The New Yorker*, "Talk of the Town" farewell on August 7, 1937, and subsequent move to Maine.

1938 *The Fox of Peapack and Other Poems*; began "One Man's Meat" column for *Harper's Magazine*.

1939 *Quo Vadimus*

1941 *A Subtreasury of American Humor*, edited with K. S. White.

1942 *One Man's Meat*.

1945 *Stuart Little*.

1946 *The Wild Flag*.

1948 Dartmouth, University of Maine, and Yale honorary degrees.

1949 *Here Is New York*.

1950 Bowdoin College honorary degree.

1952 *Charlotte's Web*; Hamilton honorary degree.

1953 Newbery honor for *Charlotte's Web*.

1954 *The Second Tree from the Corner*; Harvard, Colby honorary degrees.

1959 *The Elements of Style* (Strunk & White).

1960 Gold Medal for Essays and Criticism from the National Institute of Letters.

1962 *The Points of My Compass*.

1963 Presidential Medal of Freedom from President John F. Kennedy (presented by Maine's Senator Edmund Muskie in 1964).

1970 *Trumpet of the Swan*; Laura Ingalls Wilder Medal.

1971 National Medal for Literature.

1973 Elected to the American Academy of Arts and Letters.

1976 *The Letters of E. B. White*, edited by Dorothy Lobrano Guth.

1977 *Essays of E. B. White*; death of Katharine Sergeant White, after nearly forty-eight years of marriage.

1978 Pultizer Prize special citation for letters.

1979 *Onward and Upward in the Garden* by Katharine S. White (edited and with an introduction by E. B. White).

1981 *Poems & Sketches of E. B. White*.

1984 *E. B. White: A Biography* by Scott Elledge.

1985, October 1 Death of E. B. White at his home in North Brooklin, Maine.

1990 *E. B. White, Writings from* The New Yorker, *1925–1976*, edited by Rebecca M. Dale.

1996 *White on White*, audio recording of E. B. White selections, read by Joel White.

2006 *The Letters of E. B. White*, Revised Edition, Martha White, editor.

2011 *In the Words of E. B. White, Quotations from America's Most Companionable of Writers*, edited by Martha White.

E. B. WHITE

on

DOGS

The New Yorker, April 20, 1929
The Talk of the Town
Notes and Comment

DOG'S LIFE

A little city-bred beagle, that had been beagling all by himself in Central Park, emerged from the Ninetieth Street exit into Fifth Avenue just as we happened by. Nose to the pavement, he darted out into the traffic, looking for rabbits. The cop very kindly ushered him through to the other curb, whereupon the beagle turned around and started back. Again the cop helped him safely across.

By this time the delightful animal was perfectly sure that the rabbit was hiding between the moving lanes of cars in the middle of the Avenue, and for the next five minutes he searched thoroughly, under Yellow taxis, under Lincoln towncars, in and out. The cop, a little weary of playing the Good Samaritan, finally blew a sudden whistle and a large touring car jammed on its brakes and stopped within an inch of the pup. Motioning the bewildered driver to the curb, the officer picked up the preoccupied dog and carried him over to the car.

"That was mighty white of you, old man," said the cop. "I'm mighty grateful. I'm so grateful to you I'm going to *give* you this dog."

The motorist took him. You got to take dogs cops give you.

James Thurber's Scotty puppies, including young Daisy

The New Yorker, August 10, 1929
The Talk of the Town
Notes and Comment

COD-LIVER OIL

When our little dog Daisy seemed poorly last week, we took her down to the Ellin Prince Speyer Hospital to get some professional advice on cod-liver oil. The visit was a disarming experience; it gave us a renewed sense of the benevolence of humanity as well as the dignity of animals. The reception room, white and sterile; the reception lady, starched and kindly; the other patients, soft-eyed and wet-nosed; the phone calls, "He has no temperature today!" were all part of a strong impression that this was the nicest place in New York. And when our turn came, and we ushered Daisy into the examination room and were greeted by a doctor who wore gray spats, it was too much happiness. Even Daisy was impressed, and took a turn for the better.

The New Yorker, January 25, 1930
The Talk of the Town
Notes and Comment

ARRESTED FOR THE SINS OF DAISY

We were arrested last week for the sins of Daisy, who was without a muzzle when she met Patrolman Porco, badge No. 10020, in front of 1 Fifth Avenue. Patrolman Porco had a summons book in his hand, and no eye for Daisy's blandishments. Next morning we paid a two-dollar fine in the Third District Magistrate's Court, Second Avenue and Second Street, after waiting two hours and fifteen minutes. The fine was for leading a dog without a muzzle, in violation of the Sanitary Code. We take this opportunity to point out to William McAdoo, Patrolman Porco, Magistrate Dodge, and the clerk of the court, that while we were waiting in court to answer the charge, four garbage cans on the street in plain view from the courtroom window were visited by seven dogs of varying sizes and descriptions, not one of which wore a muzzle or even a collar, and not one of which had Daisy's charm of manner. We further point out that the railing of the courtroom and the floor under the seats violated the Sanitary Code most grossly, because they were unbelievably dirty. We merely point out these things because we wish to be a good citizen—as does Daisy, when she isn't busy looking for things under the davenport.

The New Yorker, March 1, 1930
The Talk of the Town
Notes and Comment

Anti-Muzzle Agitation

Speaking purely as a person who has never been bitten by a dog (particularly by a city dog) we approve of the anti-muzzle agitation of the S. P. C. A. We are, in fact, a rabid anti-muzzlemite. There are other and bigger problems, though, that remain to be solved in dog-walking circles. Anyone who has ever walked a dog on a leash in town—even though he's only done it once out of kindness for a sick friend—knows how badly we need an ordinance governing the conduct of two dogs who meet and want to talk things over. What about rubber leashes, so the owners of the dogs can go right on?

From *The Letters of E. B. White,* Revised Edition:
When Mrs. Angell joined the staff of The New Yorker *in August 1925, she realized that her marriage was breaking up. She had taken the editorial job partly to keep her mind off problems at home and partly to develop some skills against the day when she might have to be self-supporting. There were two children now—Roger was born in 1920. In the winter of [early] 1929, with the magazine celebrating its fourth birthday, she moved out of her house on the Upper East Side and took an apartment at 16 East 8th Street; and when summer arrived she went to Reno for a divorce. On November 13, she married E. B. White. They were both back at their desks the next day, preferring to delay until springtime the honeymoon they planned in Bermuda.*

Although they had been aware of their growing attachment to each other long before her divorce became final, the courtship was not smooth. White, always wary of entanglements, found himself in love with an

older woman, mother of two. Katharine, with her New England back-
ground, was reluctant to accept the failure of her first marriage and was
concerned about the problems a divorce and remarriage would create for
her children, and whether marriage to White made sense anyway, con-
sidering the disparity in their ages. Finally, they managed to shed their
anxieties long enough to drive out to Bedford Village, New York, and get
married in the Presbyterian church on the village green. They had told
no one of their plan, for fear the news would start an endless round of
debates. Only Katharine's dog, Daisy, went along as an attendant.
White, who hated ritualistic occasions of all kinds, remembered the cer-
emony with pleasure. "It was a very nice wedding—nobody threw any-
thing, and there was a dog fight."

He later added: "I soon realized I had made no mistake in my choice
of a wife. I was helping her pack an overnight bag one afternoon when
she said, 'Put in some tooth twine.' I knew then that a girl who called
dental floss tooth twine was the girl for me. It had been a long search,
but it was worth it."

This letter, on the occasion of Katharine's pregnancy with their son,
Joel, used Katharine's Scotty, Daisy, to speak on behalf of White.

LETTER TO KATHARINE S. WHITE

[Bedford Village, N.Y.]
[Spring 1930]

Dear Mrs. White:
I like having Josephine[1] here in the morning, although I suppose
I will get less actual thinking done—as I used to do my thinking
mornings in the bathroom. White has been stewing around for
two days now, a little bit worried because he is not sure that he
has made you realize how glad he is that there is to be what the
column writer in the Mirror calls a blessed event. So I am taking

Katharine S. White with infant Joel in the pram and Daisy on a leash,
New York City, 1931

this opportunity, Mrs. White, to help him out to the extent of writing you a brief note which I haven't done in quite a long time but have been a little sick myself as you know. Well, the truth is White is beside himself and would have said more about it but is holding himself back, not wanting to appear ludicrous to a veteran mother. What he feels, he told me, is a strange queer tight little twitchy feeling around the inside of his throat whenever he thinks that something is happening which will require so much love and all on account of you being so wonderful. (I am not making myself clear I am afraid, but on the occasions when White has spoken privately with me about this he was in no condition to make himself clear either and I am just doing the best I can in my own way.) I know White so well that I always know what is the matter with him, and it always comes to the same thing—he gets thinking that nothing that he writes or says ever quite expresses his feeling, and he worries about his inarticulateness just the same as he does about his bowels, except it is worse, and it makes him either mad, or sick, or with a prickly sensation in the head. But my, my, my, last Sunday he was so full of this matter which he couldn't talk about, and he was what Josephine in her simple way would call hoppy, and particularly so because it seemed so good that everything was starting at once—I mean those things, whatever they are, that are making such a noise over in the pond by Palmer Lewis's house,[2] and the song sparrow that even I could hear from my confinement in the house, and those little seeds that you were sprinkling up where the cut glass and bones used to be—all starting at the same time as the baby, which he seems to think exists already by the way he stands around staring at you and muttering little prayers. Of course he is also very worried for fear you will get the idea that he is regarding you merely as a future mother and not as a present person, or that he wants a child merely as a vindication of his vanity. I doubt if those things are true; White enjoys animal husbandry of all kinds including his own; and as for his regard for you, he has told me that, quite apart from this fertility, he admires you in all kinds of situations or dilemmas, some of which he says have been quite dirty.

Well, Mrs. White, I expect I am tiring you with this long letter, but as you often say yourself, a husband and wife should tell each other about the things that are on their mind, otherwise you get nowhere, and White didn't seem to be able to tell you about his happiness, so thought I would attempt to put in a word.

White is getting me a new blanket, as the cushion in the bathroom is soiled.

Lovingly,

Daisy

1 Josephine Buffa, the cook, a North Italian woman who was crazy about puppies. According to White, she was the only person he ever knew who, when a dog got sick on the floor and she had to clean up the mess, felt sorry for the dog.
2 Palmer Lewis owned the cottage the Whites had rented in Bedford Village so they would have a place in the country to take Nancy and Roger on weekends.

The New Yorker, May 24, 1930
The Talk of the Town
Notes and Comment

KICKED OUT OF SCHRAFFT'S

Daisy has it in for Mr. Shattuck. Of all places to be kicked out of, Schrafft's is the most humiliating to a Scotch terrier. "I've been kicked out of better joints than this," she said to us, under her breath, as we went through the door. The manager breathed a sigh of relief. He was such a worrier, that manager; and all for nothing. There are pleasant restaurants downtown where Daisy is one of the welcome, if unlawful, guests, and where she is admired of all eyes. In those places, sitting by our side in quiet violation of a city ordinance, she enjoys life to the full. But at Schrafft's, smuggled in and placed inconspicuously under the table, she detected a faint aura of legality and respectability about the place, and it made her restless. We don't mean that she made any fuss; we merely mean that when, discovered and dismissed, we finally gathered up our things and left during the meat course, we plainly heard her say: "Very well, then, let's get the hell out of here."

The New Yorker, December 6, 1930

DOG AROUND THE BLOCK

Dog around the block, sniff,
Hydrant sniffing, corner, grating,
Sniffing, always, starting forward,
Backward, dragging, sniffing backward,
Leash at taut, leash at dangle,
Leash in people's feet entangle—
Sniffing dog, apprised of smellings,
Love of life, and fronts of dwellings,
Meeting enemies,
Loving old acquaintance, sniff,
Sniffing hydrant for reminders,
Leg against the wall, raise,
Leaving grating, corner greeting,
Chance for meeting, sniff, meeting,
Meeting, telling, news of smelling,
Nose to tail, tail to nose,
Rigid, careful, pose,
Liking, partly liking, hating,

Then another hydrant, grating,
Leash at taut, leash at dangle,
Tangle, sniff, untangle,
Dog around the block, sniff.

—E. B. W.

The New Yorker, January 10, 1931

INTERVIEW WITH DAISY

"Well, he's gone," said Daisy cheerfully, after Mr. Caldwell had departed. "We got rid of him nice."

"*We?*" I snapped. "What do you mean *we* got rid of him? *You* got rid of him. And why? Because he dropped his cigarette case. All that fuss because a friend of mine drops his cigarette case."

Daisy pushed her two front paws straight out in front of her. "How did I know it was a cigarette case?" she said. "It might have been a rod."

"Ridiculous. Caldwell is an old friend."

"He never was at the apartment before. I should sit around on my tail while a total stranger pulls a rod on us!"

"It was a cigarette case," I said, wearily.

"Well, I couldn't see. I was sitting way the hell and gone across the. . . ."

"Quiet!" I commanded. "Either you talk decently or you go back in the bathroom on your cushion."

"Okay," said Daisy. "As far as Caldwell goes, I didn't act so bad. You take a total stranger who drops his rod, and . . ."

"Cigarette case," I corrected.

". . . and I would ordinarily give him the ankle number. I didn't give Caldwell the ankle number, I just gave him the low growl and the steady look. Anybody who makes an unusual noise gets the low growl and the steady look. That's final. It's the way I am."

"Well, I wish you'd concentrate on my objectionable guests. I happen to like Caldwell."

"He's all right," said Daisy. "A little on the dull side, maybe."

"You mean he doesn't smell like the iceman. Well, neither do I, for that matter, and you don't think I'm dull."

"Some people do," said Daisy, yawning. "And speaking of the iceman, life is what you make it. If I had a chipmunk in the apartment I might adopt a different attitude toward tradespeople. I give the iceman my ankle number not because it does anything to him, but because it does something to me."

"It does something to all of us," I sneered. "It bores us all to tears. There'll be no chipmunks, either. This apartment is confusing enough without chipmunks. Besides, what's the matter with the little rubber dog that Mrs. Newberry brought you from Paris—it makes a squeaking noise like a chipmunk. You can shake that all you darn please."

"Can't I, though. If you knew what it costs me to throw myself into the spirit of rubber toys! It takes a lot out of a dog. I had a grandmother in the old country who bit the pants off an earl, the elegant bitch, and now it's come to rubber toys. You must admit, though, that the Scottish terrier approaches rubber toys with his eyes open—you have to hand the breed that."

"On the other hand, I sometimes think you approach a lot of things with your mind shut. I've never understood, for example, why you discriminate between our iceman, whom you meet informally here in the apartment, and the doorman of One Fifth Avenue, whom you meet ceremoniously on the street. Where do you draw the line? Both are honest working people, both are grotesquely dressed—why do you resent the one and cultivate the other?"

"You wouldn't understand," replied Daisy. "The doorman is the symbol of majesty—possibly that's it. I have to have that, even though I see through it, just as some men have to have a pretty girl even though they see through her. Don't throw One Fifth Avenue in my face—I go in with my eyes open. Besides, it seems to me I'm getting to be something of a symbol myself. I know what's going on. The Scottish terrier has been exploited in an unbridled manner: Scotty pins, Scotty buckles, Scotty hat ornaments, Scotty Kiddie Pants, Scotties on the bathmat, Scotties in the Texaco ads, wooden Scotties on suburban lawns. It's a crime the way we've been taken up. When I meet another Scotch dòg on the street now we both feel like a couple of Elks (and I've met some I wouldn't be found dead with, too)."

"Yes, I've noticed that," I replied bitterly.

"It's a cock-eyed country," Daisy continued, "and it's the same all along the line. I know what's going on. Everything gets taken over by big business, I don't care what line you're in. Look at President Hoover: he makes some crazy scrawls with his pencil while he's answering the telephone and a concern gets hold of the design and brings out the Hoover Scribble Rompers for little folks. Hell, the President and I are in the same boat."

"You're talking awful big," I said.

"I'm feeling awful big," said Daisy. "Where's that rubber dog?"

LETTER TO KATHARINE S. WHITE

Rockingham Hotel
Portsmouth, N.H.
[June 27, 1931]
Saturday night

Dear K:
We are camped here for the night, Daisy and Mrs. L. in their Sink

of Loneliness, #37; I in quieter diggings one flight up. The two women dined in their room, as the expedient solution of their special wants: a pot of tea and a beef bone. I dined alone in the Oak Room, below. This being my first major trip with a terrier and a domestic, I have got along fairly well—thus far the chief difficulty is that they roam away from the main body and are found far afield, fooling with each other. It is as hard to catch Mrs. L. in a field of buttercups as it is to catch a butterfly.

Luncheon (at Stafford Springs) was a great personal triumph, if not a moral victory. The restaurant insisted that the dog be tied outside, to a tree. Mrs. L. would hear of no such arrangement— said Daisy would be prostrated with fright and loneliness, the little darlin', and insisted that I eat my lunch while she waited outside with D. and then I could wait with Daisy while she ate. It was clear to me that a double-shift arrangement like that would increase our running time to about two weeks; but Mrs. L. was adamant. Luckily I discovered a table so situated that Daisy could be tied on the porch yet separated from Mrs. L. by only the thickness of a screen door. This worked perfectly.

The two of them have just passed through the lobby on their way out for their evening walk. It is raining, and D. is constipated by travel, I suspect—so they will probably be back about midnight.

Also registered at the Rockingham is a span of Cairns.
See you Tuesday—Love,
Andy

13

The New Yorker, March 12, 1932
(Also printed in *Quo Vadimus*)

Obituary

Daisy ("Black Watch Debatable") died December 22, 1931, when she was hit by a Yellow Cab in University Place. At the moment of her death she was smelling the front of a florist's shop. It was a wet day, and the cab skidded up over the curb—just the sort of excitement that would have amused her, had she been at a safe distance. She is survived by her mother, Jeannie; a brother, Abner; her father, whom she never knew; and two sisters, whom she never liked. She was three years old. Daisy was born at 65 West Eleventh Street in a clothes closet at two o'clock of a December morning in 1928. She came, as did her sisters and brothers, as an unqualified surprise to her mother, who had for several days previously looked with a low-grade suspicion on the box of bedding that had been set out for the delivery, and who had gone into the clothes closet merely because she had felt funny and wanted a dark, awkward place to feel funny in. Daisy was the smallest of the litter of seven, and the oddest. Her life was full of incident but not of accomplishment. Persons who knew her only slightly regarded her as an opinionated little bitch, and said so; but she had a small circle of friends who saw through her, cost what it did. At Speyer hospital, where she used to go when she was indisposed, she was known as "Whitey," because, the man told me, she was black. All her life she was subject to moods, and her feeling about horses laid her sanity open to question. Once she slipped her leash and chased a horse for three blocks through heavy traffic, in the carking belief that she was an effective agent against horses. Drivers of teams, seeing her only in the moments of her delirium, invariably leaned far out of their seats and gave tongue, mocking her; and thus made themselves even more ridiculous, for the moment, than Daisy.

She had a stoical nature, and spent the latter part of her life an invalid, owing to an injury to her right hind leg. Like many invalids, she developed a rather objectionable cheerfulness, as though to deny that she had cause for rancor. She also developed, without instruction or encouragement, a curious habit of holding people firmly by the ankle without actually biting them—a habit that gave her an immense personal advantage and won her many enemies. As far as I know, she never even broke the thread of a sock, so delicate was her grasp (like a retriever's), but her point of view was questionable, and her attitude was beyond explaining to the person whose ankle was at stake. For my own amusement, I often tried to diagnose this quirkish temper, and I think I understand it: she suffered from a chronic perplexity, and it relieved her to take hold of something.

She was arrested once, by Patrolman Porco. She enjoyed practically everything in life except motoring, an exigency to which she submitted silently, without joy, and without nausea. She never grew up, and she never took pains to discover, conclusively, the things that might have diminished her curiosity and spoiled her taste. She died sniffing life, and enjoying it.

LETTER TO KATHARINE S. WHITE

[January? 1933]
[Interoffice memo]

Dear Mrs. White—
Sympathizing with you in your recent dilemma when you found yourself sandwiched in between two old-line coupon clippers, and aware of your humiliation, I made so bold as to seek out the enclosed pamphlet from the Fifth Avenue Bank, explaining how

such embarrassments may be avoided—at a slight charge. A cheerful fire was burning in the hearth, and it was warm and cozy inside the Bank even though I was immediately under suspicion because of my odd clothes. I do not know that it is at all necessary for you to have a Custody Account, but what with Mrs. Lardner so sick and Willy [Buffa] growing up and Daisy dead[1] and Nancy off to school and Joe's cough and everything I didn't know but what you might like to consider it. Ever since I found the railroad tickets in with the sliced bananas and yesterday's melons, I have wondered.[2]

Yrs lovingly,

Mr. White

1 Daisy was run over on December 22, 1931, by a Yellow Cab that jumped the curb at the corner of University Place and 8th Street. Mrs. Lardner, who had been walking the dog and who loved her dearly, was so upset by the accident that she left the Whites' employ. An account of Daisy's death appears in "Obituary," a *New Yorker* piece later included in *Quo Vadimus?*

2 Katharine White had once absent-mindedly thrown the family's Maine-to-New York railway tickets in the garbage pail. A search of the local dump followed, and the tickets were recovered.

The New Yorker, April 1, 1933
The Talk of the Town
Notes and Comment
(Also in *Writings from* The New Yorker, *1925–1976*)

Dog Eat Dog

Most imperative of recent missives was a letter from *Forbes*, reminding us that we are not a bluebird. "You are not a bluebird," the letter said, gruffly, and then added, "you are a business man." There was a kind of finality about this news, and we read on.

"Business is a hard, cold-blooded game today. Survival of the fittest. Dog eat dog. Produce or get out. A hundred men are after your job." If *Forbes* only knew it, goading of this sort is the wrong treatment for us. We are not, as they say, a bluebird. Nobody who reads the *Nation* regularly, as we do, can retain his amateur bluebird standing. As for business, we agree that it is a hard, cold-blooded game. Survival of the fittest. Dog eat dog. The fact that about eighty-five per cent of the dogs have recently been eaten by the other dogs perhaps explains what long ago we noticed about business: that it had a strong smell of boloney. If dog continues to eat dog, there will be only one dog left, and he will be sick to his stomach.

The New Yorker, February 24, 1934
The Talk of the Town
Notes and Comment

DOG SHOW: THE SCOTTISH TERRIER

The memorable thing about the Dog Show was the booing of the Scottish terrier. We watched a team of four Scotties take a blue ribbon, and heard the garden roar its disapproval. A fickle land, with styles in dogs changing along with styles in dresses! The Scottish terrier achieved a fame such as no breed ever dreamed of, and then was victimized by its own national advertising. Public favor has swung over toward the more rangy breeds, dogs with legs. Setters are the adored of show-goers. Bedlingtons are popular with people of fashion, who seek the unusual and who would rather be seen dead than leading anything as common as a Scotty. It is all very sad. As the one-time owner of a Scottish terrier, whose memory we hold green, we wish to apologize to Gleniffer Ideal, Ramoon Certainty, Gleniffer Glad Eye, and Gleniffer Frivolity, for the rudeness of the spectators. To hear, in the short space of one week, a Scottish terrier booed by an audience and President Roosevelt criticized by Charles Lindbergh[1] was a great strain on our nerves. The props of life seem to be crumbling fast.

1 *Newsweek Magazine* had made public a telegram in which Charles Lindbergh criticized the President for his handling of the so-called Air Mail scandal, which had resulted in the U.S. Army Air Corps taking over the delivery of airmail routes in 1934.

LETTER TO ALEXANDER WOOLLCOTT[1]

25 West 45th Street
November [1934?]

Dear Friend and Reader:
Thanks for the ad over the wireless. I have a spaniel that defrocked a nun last week. He took hold of the cord. I had hold of the leash. It was like elephants holding tails.
Imagine me undressing a nun, even second hand.
Yrs,
E. B. White

1 Alexander Woollcott was a critic and commentator for *The New Yorker*. His book of theater articles, *Shouts and Murmurs* (1922) became the name for his *New Yorker* column, and the magazine has more recently reused the title for humorous pieces in general.

The New Yorker, January 19, 1935
The Talk of the Town
Notes and Comment

IN THE CLUTCHES OF AN IRISH TERRIER

A young couple we know are in the clutches of an Irish terrier. The animal, a young male, is fairly decent around the apartment except for one eccentricity: he won't let even his best friend touch the bed he sleeps on—a soft Abercrombie cushion much in vogue among degenerate city canines. He quietly but firmly offers to tear to pieces anybody who so much as reaches out a hand toward this bed. The husband of the family, who likes to think of himself in a general way as the dog's master, is fed up with this treacherous performance and is ready to give the pup the beating of his life; but the lady of the house, who has read more books and things, has decided that the bed has a sexual fascination for the dog because it had once been occupied by a female terrier who presumably left a few hairpins and powder around. She says you can't blame a dog for defending what to him is the very symbol of femininity. Nevertheless, the situation is a bad one; every move either one of them makes to touch the bed, either for sanitary or purely whimsical or experimental reasons, is met by a savagery almost unbelievable in Man's Best Friend. The husband's temper is up; he feels that life in this city is abortive and unnatural enough without the added complication of a dog who is in love with his own bed.

The New Yorker, February 23, 1935
The Talk of the Town
Notes and Comment

Dog Show: A New Showmanship

Next year, when Dog Show time comes round, we would like to see a wholly new brand of showmanship introduced into the Garden. We were horribly bored by the judging last week—all that business of standing around a ring, hour after hour, brushing a dog's hair the wrong way and jacking his tail up with the palm of your hand. Who cares, anyway? Only a handful of fanciers know about a dog's points, and besides, conformation and ring manners are piffling qualities in a dog, revealing little about the animal's character, exploits, or temper. A dog should be made to work for his ribbon, each breed in his own wise. Pointers should have to point, Shepherds should be required to herd a band of sheep from the east goal to the west goal. Poodles should be required to jump through a paper hoop, not just follow Mrs. Sherman Hoyt around the ring. English bull terriers should be made to count up to ten, retrievers retrieve rubber ducks, Scotties chew up old shoes. Greyhounds should be put over the high hurdles. Sled dogs should race with a little anti-toxin, while St. Bernards carry brandy to anyone in the audience who feels weak, preferably us. Beagles would jolly well have to beagle, or shut up. How about it, dogs—are you dogs, or mice?

The New Yorker, May 18, 1935
The Talk of the Town
Notes and Comment

TICK-HUNTING

Things go in waves. This has been a great year for children's diseases—even adults breaking out suddenly in the middle of a dinner party, with measles, mumps, chicken pox, or scarlet fever. More alarming to us, however, is the prevalence of ticks, which fasten themselves to dogs. The city is full of them. So acute is the epidemic that the Ellin Prince Speyer Hospital for animals has refused to accept, for hospitalization, any tick-infested applicant. We spent the greater part of this week deticking the faithful guardian of our home, who is a setup for ticks if ever there was one. (He eats chewing gum.) We gained a little ground, but it is just a beginning; tick-hunting is no fad, it is a career. Our summer is all cut out for us; we can see that, and so can the dog. He is beginning to wear that patient look around the eyes.

The New Yorker, September 14, 1935
The Talk of the Town
Notes and Comment

THE SPAN, THE TANDEM, THE FOUR-IN-HAND

In the dark days of 1932, the well-dressed woman wore, among other things, one wire-haired terrier in leash. It becomes increasingly apparent that the styles are changing and enlarging: today, the span, the tandem, the four-in-hand are the vogue. Braces of spaniels, couples of dachshunds, and platoons of poodles make strolling an art, both for the dog owner and for the unattached pedestrian. A lady who leads (or is led by) only one animal appears shabby. We welcome the trend; it's a pleasure to see families becoming skilled again in the use of their hands. It is no mean feat to drive three spaniels, after they've been shut up in the kitchenette all night.

Incidentally, although we have no figures to back us up, it seems to us that the Pekinese is coming back. We are glad of this. The Peke is a most grossly maligned breed. Associated by fate with dowagers and ladies in fur neckpieces, this valiant animal with the big round eyes and the churlish mouth has never impressed the world with his true character. We have known one or two Pekes, and they had gaiety and courage. What the breed needs is to be plucked, and given a chance in some field trials, preferably in rather open, rolling country where clearance is not important.

The New Yorker, March 14, 1936
The Talk of the Town
Notes and Comment

CANINE CATERING COMPANY

The Harvard community has written, en masse, to assure us that Sherman Hall, where the Baby's Dy-dee Service pays clandestine calls, harbors two legitimate babies—a boy and a girl. The tots belong to faculty members who, when they leased the apartments, were given to understand that there were to be no children, but found Nature even more compelling than Harvard.

Incidentally, Glass Hall, a twin of Sherman, is regularly served not by the Dy-dee outfit but by the Canine Catering Company—balanced meals for particular puppies. Thus is the higher life made easier, if not higher.

The New Yorker, March 14, 1936
The Talk of the Town
Notes and Comment

HAWTHORNE HOUNDS

A while ago we read a stirring little newspaper article by Albert Payson Terhune, sonorously captioned "They Always Get Their Man," all about the exploits of the three bloodhounds belonging to Troop K of the State Police. It was a pair of these hounds which found Grover Whalen, Jr., lying unconscious at the bottom of a ravine near his brother's estate at Dobbs Ferry, after hundreds of human searchers had failed. Now, we yield to no Terhune in our admiration for bloodhounds, so last week we journeyed out to Hawthorne, just north of White Plains, and visited the kennels at Troop K headquarters. They are in charge of Captain Christopher Kemmler, who has commanded Troop K these past four years. Captain Kemmler introduced us to his charges: Queenie (black and tan, and none too stylish); Red, her brother (reddish-brown and handsome, with fine russet eyes); and the most recent acquisition, a bitch named Sappo. "Sappo?" we asked Captain Kemmler. "*Sappo,*" he said. Sappo is just a good, all-around bloodhound, but Queenie and Red both have their specialties and sort of divide up the work; she's a whiz at picking up trails, and he has the best record following them up, making "finds." They get a light workout three or four times a week. A trooper wanders a few miles into the Hawthorne hinterland, and the hounds trail him. "They have never failed to get their man," the Captain ter-huned. "Their record is perfect."

Until two years ago, Troop K did all its man-hunting with police dogs borrowed from a neighboring private kennel. They set a pretty good record trailing lost children, escaped criminals, and the like. Police dogs are smarter than bloodhounds, Captain

Kemmler admits, even if their sense of smell leaves something to be desired. The troopers began using hounds when the police-dog kennel closed down, and they have traced numerous stray, befuddled folk, but haven't taken part in any criminal cases. The cops feel a little sheepish about this. Captain Kemmler trains them not to bay on the trail; that sort of thing, however dramatic, would only warn a fleeing criminal, or frighten a lost child. Like all admirers of bloodhounds, Captain Kemmler is annoyed by the Uncle-Tom's-Cabin legend of their viciousness; they're gentle as kittens, he says. As far as he knows, Troop K's bloodhounds are the only ones in New York State Police, but he thinks other states may have some. The hounds are all perfectly affable and happy, getting along fine with one another and with the troopers who take care of them. The Captain told us that Red had lately discovered that the boiler-room was much more comfortable than his outdoor run, and had several times succeeded in sneaking off for naps beside the furnace. That's positively the only rift in Troop K's bloodhound lute, though. "Not a very serious fault," we remarked. "No," said the Captain.

We thought it might be instructive to see an expert blood-hound at work, and timidly offered ourself as the quarry. The Captain summoned a sergeant, who put a harness and leash on Red. Then, leaving our glove with the Captain, we went off down the road, and, after circling about several times, in order to make things hard, hid in a shed. Nothing happened for a while; then we heard sounds of the chase, which surprisingly, grew fainter instead of stronger. We peeked out, and saw Red, dragging the sergeant by the leash, and followed by the Captain, tearing down a totally different road from the one we had taken; his ears were flapping, and he acted as if the end of the trail was near. We went back to the kennels and waited. Pretty soon the Captain and the sergeant appeared, dragging Red, who slid along with all four feet stuck out in rebellion. He was baying mournfully. "Oh, *there* you are," said the Captain. "Yes, Where have you been?" we said. "Boiler-room," said the Captain peevishly, handing back our glove.

The New Yorker, August 15, 1936
The Talk of the Town
Notes and Comment

VOGUE ON DOGS

Ordinarily, we don't insist that a person, or a magazine, be consistent. But we are disturbed, just the same, by Vogue, whose attitude about life seems suddenly to be coming apart. We have been studying the latest issue, as is our wont, and while ninety-nine per cent of it is still devoted to the proposition that the female should make herself irresistibly alluring to the male, there has crept into one section of Vogue a note which suggests a wholly conflicting philosophy. There is, specifically, a little notice (you will find it under the dog department) which announces a product known as "Cupid Chaser"—a substance to be administered to a bitch in season. The purpose of it is to rob her of her charm and make her positively offensive to dogs. We are amazed to find Vogue in such a complete about-face.

Letter to Katharine S. White

[North Brooklin, Maine]
[September 3, 1936]
Thursday night

Dear Kay:

The great stillness has at last descended. Nancy and Roger departed directly after supper, in charge of Bill Schnauzer and Buster. They were headed for the Boston train via the Dirigo Theatre. I believe a bevy, or cluster, of Roger's female friends are expected at the station to see him off. Tunney [Roger's bulldog] is moody, with waves of nausea overcoming him at rather short intervals.

We had a fine, soft rain all last night, steady and wet. Everything was thoroughly drenched at last, including the priming coat on the fence. It still rained this morning, and Joe and I went over to Center Harbor and boarded *Astrid* to ease the lines. Nance and I sailed her around yesterday morning, lunching aboard and arriving in time for the race.[1] The race, incidentally, turned into quite an affair. There was a flat calm at the start, with the boats unable to drift across the line, all jammed together, panting for a puff. They hung that way for about five minutes, then the wind backed into the south and began to blow hard, rippling the Reach into a lovely sun-flecked turmoil. The Beasts sprang away, and Nance cracked up almost immediately, her rudder-track pulling out. The committee boat towed her in, and then went out to salvage the rest of the fleet. All but three managed to complete one lap, and then turned tail and ran into the harbor. It was a brisk sight; even the harbor was all chopped up with white caps, and in the midst of everything, in ran the *Mattie* under full press of sail and rounded to off the old steamboat wharf. She looked alarmingly spruced up, and it turns out she has been all re-commissioned and is now a pleasure boat, out of Camden. How are the mighty fallen![2] Nancy was quite disappointed about not finishing her last race of the season, but was sort of glad to be in the harbor. Dick Emery was indignant that the race was called after one lap, and feels that the Haven fleet is growing soft. . . .

Joe is well and is turning over in his mind an invitation to a picnic supper at the Sturtevants on Saturday. Mrs. S. and Peter were by this P.M., and Peter remained for a visit. Ros and John and Jane [Newberry] came to tea, bringing me a book and carrying away three. According to Rosamond, John is very anxious to play tennis. I am invited to South Brooksville with Joe for luncheon on Monday. Fanny laid an egg on Tuesday, and again this morning. She uses the north stall this year, rather than the south. Greater privacy. The cock has disappeared entirely, after an affair with Freddy.[3] I horsewhipped Fred and banished him to the garage, but he seems keen and ready to go.

Joe's latest literary passion is a Camel ad in the funny paper, called "Mysteries of the Undersea World." It is all about a deep sea diver, whose digestive processes are improved by addiction to a Certain Brand of cigarette. I had to read it four times tonight, and then had to play the piano loud after Joe went to bed, so the undersea creatures would swim out of his thoughts. He announced today that he wanted to write letters, but then said that it was impossible to do it without you.

The woods and sea are beginning to close in already. The blue heron fishes daily at the frogpond. Darkness falls with the meat course. Joe and I have gathered boughs of red swamp maple, to decorate the back porch. Last Tuesday in a strong westerly the Bemis sloop dragged its mooring clear across the harbor and brought up on the mud. Mrs. B. [Chapey] got her off, with some local assistance. No damage. Madeline's food has been very good, with a strong trend to meat balls—or what Joe calls lamb chops.[4] My health has been good, but I don't sleep at night because for some reason I can't breathe when I lie down. Whether this is climate, heart, or an uncured feather pillow, I can't seem to determine.

Lots of love from us all, & my best to the Northamptonians.

Andy

1 Center Harbor Yacht Club fleet's semiweekly race. The Beasts were Brutal Beasts, small sloops designed by Starling Burgess.

2 The *Mattie* was a coasting schooner, built to carry lumber and firewood.

3 A red dachshund. White had bought Fred as a puppy in a Madison Avenue pet shop. His AKC papers, White always thought, had been forged. He was a large, strong-willed, beer-drinking dog about whom much has been written by his master. Katharine White loved dachshunds, but her husband's feelings about the breed were mixed. "For a number of years," he wrote, "I have been agreeably encumbered by a very large and dissolute dachshund named Fred. . . . He even disobeys me when I instruct him in something that he wants to do. And when I answer his peremptory scratch at the door and hold the door open for him to walk through, he stops in the middle to light a cigarette, just to hold me up." Fred died at thirteen, "of his excesses and after a drink of brandy."

4 Madeline Day, a high-school girl, came to the Whites as extra help during her summer vacation. She is now Mrs. Roy Snow, proprietress of a Blue Hill boutique.

The New Yorker, October 10, 1936
The Talk of the Town
Notes and Comment

THE DOG HAS HAD HIS DAY

The bitter pill that is Sunday afternoon had stuck halfway down our throat; the living room, colliding with time itself, sprawled at our feet, a foul mass of half-read supplements. Mechanically we

E. B. White holding the young pup, Fred—"the Cecil B. DeMille of dogs."

stumbled on into the book section and began reading a review of a volume of poems by Prokosch. "And here, also, are those manifestations of a dying civilization—superstition, perversion, nostalgia, defeatism—in symbol and image." We gazed mournfully out of the window. A leaf wrenched itself loose from a small, sickly tree, spun to the pavement. "Man has had his day," we read, turning back to the review. The paper slipped from our grasp and fluttered to the moldering carpet. We fell into a deep, dreamless sleep.

Next morning, the theme recurred: we couldn't get it out of our head that man had had his day. Normally it is our pleasure to defend the noble destiny of the race, at least through breakfast; but this time we just couldn't carry it off. In the middle of orange juice a phone call came from a brisk lady who said it was time we came in for the semi-annual cleaning of our teeth. "Sorry," we replied, "but we have had our day. Let's stop this pretense of pro- phylaxis; everywhere we find impressions of a warm, overripe beauty, decay. Why should we try to stop decay, even in our teeth?" The lady hung up, in what seemed honest alarm, and we returned to the table to stare at a poached egg.

You wouldn't think that a sentence in a book review in a Sun- day paper could stick with us that way. The strange part was that, although the idea of man's decline affected us with an almost unbearable dolor, it also seemed to simplify our contacts with all sorts of rather difficult people. On Tuesday an inspector from the S. P. C. A. arrived, to insist that we license our dog. We shook our head. "The dog has had his day," we replied.

"What?" said the inspector.

"He's had his day," we repeated.

"You *got* a dog here, haven't you?" he asked.

"Yes," we said, "but we bought him in a pet shop and he is only one of the many evidences of bourgeois decadence you could find around the house. A dog license would be ironical indeed."

The man stared hard at us for a second, and then went away.

The thing got to the point where we felt we had to buy Prokosch's book to decide for ourself whether man had had his day. So we picked up a copy on our way to lunch Wednesday and carried it to the restaurant. We ordered liver and bacon, opened the book to the first poem, and started slowly to read:

O summon out of memory
Into understanding
So that all may fear it
From the blood and fever
Of our passionate and forever
Unregenerate spirit. . . .

At this point the restaurant proprietor, who had been fiddling with a radio, began to get the first premonitory sounds of a ball game. In another minute, the Yankee lineup wove itself inextricably into the poem:

O love
Remember Alexander
Alcibiades,
Crosetti, shortstop,
Achilles: more slender
Than the slenderest of these,
Rolfe, third base,
Yet lovelier, still more haunting
Of voice, feature and form,
Di Maggio. . . .

Our considered opinion is that poets, although the most valuable of prophets, are now and always have been hypersensitive to decadence. Their art owes a great debt to the cloying beauty of things past their prime.

A more immediate question is whether democracy has had its day. . . .

The New Yorker, December 5, 1936
The Talk of the Town
Notes and Comment

WINTER SHOW

Into Madison Square Garden, which can take any amount of punishment, will presently get dumped a large quantity of tailormade snow, for the Winter Sports Show—skiing, skating, dog racing, and that stuff. On Wednesday, December 9th, there will be a rehearsal, and from then on through the 12th there will be matinée and evening performances daily. Prices, from $.75 to 3.30.

We were sufficiently dazzled by this project to make a few desultory inquiries. The snow, we are advised, is in fact ground-up ice. You take a three-hundred-pound cake of ordinary bartender's ice, feed it into a machine run by an old Buick motor, and it comes out mashed into fine flakes. The flakes are ejected by air pressure, but there's a trick to it: if you shoot them too far through the air, even as much as thirty feet, their edges melt and they become granular, hard to ski on. A machine can make forty tons an hour, and the Garden has two machines—so winter is really no problem.

The snow will cover the floor of the arena, and the jump, to a depth of four or five inches. The slide starts near the men's room in the top gallery on the Ninth Avenue side, descends rapidly to the takeoff, and discharges the hare-brained skiers onto a fifty-five-foot landing slope in full view of everybody. They will try to stop themselves by stem-Christies and Telemarks. Below, on either side of the runout, will be an ice rink, which the skiers better not hit. There will be attractive backgrounds of igloos, spruces, tepees, and ushers, and the band is going to be disguised as a detachment of Royal Canadian Mounted Police. Two encampments of dog teams will lie dozing on the sidelines, dreaming their disagreeable dreams. There will be no Indians. All heat in the Garden will be turned off and the refrigerating plant under the floor will be kept running full blast. The management expects to get the temperature down around 26°, exclusive of New York animal heat.

The Cheseboro–Whitman Company, of Long Island City, which has the contract to put up the ski slide, has been getting in trim by doing some scaffolding jobs around Radio City. They feel fit and ready to go. Skiers will reach the top of the slide by a tramway. (Skiers are brave, but lazy.) There will be snowshoe races by French Canadians, two times around the eighth-of-a-mile track. These guys are terrific: one of them, Yvan Coutu, can do 100 yards in 10-1/5 seconds. Try it sometime, with a couple of old tennis racquets.

The dog races will be a problem, as is everything which remotely concerns dogs. First of all, they can only race dogs from the same encampment, otherwise it wouldn't be a race at all, just an old-fashioned brawl. Furthermore, they can't race the dogs more than part way around the track, because sled dogs won't go spurting by a place where they've been tethered—they want to stop and smell it, for old times' sake. The dog's attitude about this is probably right, and Man's wrong.

We asked the Garden people why, instead of making snow out of ice, they didn't just use borax for their slide. "Because that's crazy stuff," they replied, coldly.

The New Yorker, January 9, 1937
Talk of the Town
Notes and Comment

WORMS?

Seated between two intellectual giants after dinner, we were borne lightly along on conversation's wave, from country to country, dipping into problems of empire, the rise and fall of dynasties, the loves and hates of kings, the warrings in Spain, the trends in Russia, strikes, revolutions, diplomacies, the dissolution of peoples; and without a pause heard everything under the sun made plain. We have the deepest envy for anyone who can feel at home with great matters, and who, armed cap-a-pie with information, can see into the motives of rulers and the hearts of subjects, and can answer Yes to this, No to that. Our envy was so strong that when we returned home at midnight and our wife asked us whether, in our opinion, our dog had worms, we answered with a bold Yes, in a moment of vainglory, pretending that here was a thing on which we spoke knowingly—though such was far from the case, as we both secretly knew.

The New Yorker, June 26, 1937
The Talk of the Town
Notes and Comment

DOGS ARE MORE FORTHRIGHT

We lunched alone today, as is our wont. It has its peptic advantages and induces a disconsolate attitude, which has some slight literary value. Looking about the room, though, at the tables of twos, threes, and fours, we realized how important a function lunch is in New York, how drastic and purposeful. There was a dark pall of gain hanging over every table—everyone there for some reason of business or intrigue: salesmen, applicants, supplicants, agents provocateurs, contact executives, actresses gaming with managers, writers taking the temperature of editors, lovers sparring for their strange vantage, everywhere a sprig of personal increase garnishing the cold salmon. Next to us a burlap-bag man was convincing a poultry-feed gentleman that his particular sack kept the vitamins alive longer than usual. As we watched the interplay, we envisioned millions of hens standing in caked henyards, uttering the dreamy summer sound that hens make, unaware of the new sack, the new retention of vitamins in the laying mash, the myriad other new things which arise from lunch in town.

With nothing much else to do, we complained of the fish, which stank. "You do not like the fish?" said the captain, after the waiter had whispered about the trouble at his table. "It stinks," we said, in our simplest vein. But the captain would not smell it, despite the nose being the most valuable of all organs in the appraisal of food. He would bring us, without charge, another dish—but he wouldn't be caught sniffing his own fish. Dogs are more forthright in these situations. They not only will sniff bad fish, they will stick up for it.

Letter to Charles G. Muller[1]

North Brooklin, Maine
11 July 1937

Dear Charlie:
I was thirty-eight years old today, and spent most of the day trying to build a henyard—which seems an odd milestone. The

planks seemed heavy, and I noticed that I quit early and took a drink. We've been here just a week, and I haven't had a sail yet, *Astrid* having blown the bJesus out of her muffler, or what the boatyard man calls her "maximum silencer." We finally located a new maximum silencer, and she is afloat in the Benjamin River, ready to go. . . .

We've had terrifically hot weather here, and for the first time the swimming has seemed actually alluring. Eight broiling sunny days, with very light wind, if any. The pollen count has been high, and my hay fever has raged quietly all through the customary membranes. It's suicide for me to arrive here on July first, but I do it anyway. I would really rather feel bad in Maine than good anywhere else. Maybe I should warn you what a madhouse you are stepping into here. I have ten turkeys, three dogs, three children, three or four in help at the last count (including the postmaster, who grows wonderful salpiglossis and scabiosa), two water systems, a cesspool, a chimney swift, a moosehead covered with swallow crap, a frogpond, a family of bantams, a Sears Roebuck catalogue, and one hundred and sixty-five chairs. There is also a fine view of Mount Desert. Roger's old bulldog, Tunney, who is twelve and has the worst breath of any dog in Hancock County, is in love again, and goes sobbing all over the house, playing his violin. He located a Scotty bitch down on the shore last summer, and nine weeks later she underwent a Caesarian section, which my wife tells me is no fun. They spayed her while they were at it, but even that doesn't quiet our old bulldog, who apparently lives for his memories. We also have a 7-year-old 7-passenger touring car which I bought by mail this spring from a guy in Omaha, Nebraska. If you would still like to come, I hope you do.

My last stint for *The New Yorker* gets mailed on July 28th, so I'm free any time after that date, but would prefer not to go cruising till about August 1 or 2, as Nancy (Kay's daughter) who is spending this month at the Marine Biological Laboratory in

Woods Hole is arriving here the 29th or 30th, and I don't want to disappear with her favorite 30-foot boat too abruptly. I should think if you got here either Saturday or Sunday, whichever day is best for you, it would be O.K. for us. You will probably like to park your tail here for a couple of square meals, to fatten you up against *Astrid*'s diet of beer and stewed periwinkles, and then we can shove off. I have nothing in mind except to poke around this beautiful coast, do a little exploring and plenty of loafing. I don't want to be gone for more than about ten days, on account of the extra load my absence puts on Kay, but ten days ought to give us some sunshine, indolence, and derring do. . . .

Andy

1 Charles Muller was a friend from Cornell, a public relations man and author of children's books, and he and White shared a love of sailing.

Letter to James Thurber [1]

245 East 48 Street
[October? 1937]
Sunday afternoon

Dear Jim:

Sunday afternoons are about the same as when you left, people walking their dog out, and the dog not doing anything, the sky grey and terrible, and the L making the noise that you hear when you are under ether. The middle of the afternoon is the saddest time, because it is neither right after lunch nor right before supper, it is not time to have a drink yet, and if you call someone on the phone, the phone just rings. It is the time little boys come in from the garden and say that there is nothing doing out there. I got back from Maine a week ago, but all this week I have been looking around and wondering why I came away.

Katharine S. White's children: Nancy Angell (with Moses),
Roger Angell, and Joel White

I made the drive in an open car with a turkey in the back seat and a retriever in the front. Stopped off at the Coateses' and we ate the bird and freshened up the dog. Els and Bob are all right, and the valley where they live is still full of Cowleys and Blumes, as always, and the Rehacks' cows and now and then a pheasant. Bob is quitting his job doing *Time* book reviews and has started in doing an art column for the weekly *New Yorker*, where I used to work when I could think of anything to say. He is looking for a furnished apartment in town. Joe Sayre is back from the Vineyard with third act trouble. . . . McKelway is in Ford's with booze gloom. Walter Lippmann and Mrs. Lippmann are getting a divorce. Ruth Fleischmann is now Mrs. Peter Vischer, and (as Ross put it) we now have another little mouth to feed.

I saw the David Garnett piece about you. I can't think how I happened to see it but I did. I doubt if you are the most original writer living, but I doubt whether anybody is. I am the second most inactive writer living, and the third most discouraged. The greatest living writer is Morris Markey,[2] and the greatest living woman is Helen. If you want the names of the other living writers I can probably get Brayshaw to get them for you. And before I forget it, I better tell you what Josephine, who is the most original living North Italian woman, calls my Labrador retriever. She heard us calling him Moses, which is his name, but she apparently didn't quite catch the sound because she invariably addresses the dog as Mosher. "Come, Mosher, come on, naah?" Every once in a while she puts a "Mr." in front of it, and calls him Mr. Mosher. He so hoppy.

I, too, know that the individual plight is the thing. I knew it when I stayed with my mother while she died in a hospital in Georgetown. I knew it day before yesterday when Joe (looking suspiciously like me) stood up in meeting house and recited the 117th psalm before the elementary school. You beget a son when your mind is not on that at all, and seven years later he is there in a clean white shirt, praising the Lord. You spend your days chuckling at the obstinacies of French waiters and Italian cooks, but always knowing that much of life is insupportable and that no individual play can have a happy ending. If you have the poetic temperament you go on groping toward something which will express all this in a burst of choir music, and your own inarticulateness only hastens the final heart attack. Even when an artist has the ability and the strength to assemble something of the beauty and the consternation which he feels, he is usually so jealous of other artists that he has no time for pure expression.

Today with the radio yammering at you and the movies turning all human emotions into cup custard, the going is tough. Or I find it tough.

If you go to Corse, you can either take the little paqueboat from Marseilles or the plane from Antibes. I took the boat one time, stayed up all night on deck to escape the cackaroachies in the bed, and saw Ajaccio just at sunrise. I have never seen anything like that since. There is a good small hotel called Hotel des Etrangers with a pretty garden full of lizards and sweet smelling vines. I suppose there are still vines in the garden of the Hotel and that they still smell sweet. Give my regards to Victor, who will not remember me.

I passed through Litchfield, for the first time in my life, last Saturday, and bought two pairs of boxing gloves in Torrington, junior size, for the wars. It'll be nineteen years come December that I was discharged from the army. Or is it twenty? Litchfield seemed beautiful, and Tony Coates and Joe White liked the boxing gloves. All towns should have a common, sheep or no sheep. George Horace Lorimer and Osgood Perkins are dead. Lots of love to you and Helen from us'ns.

Andy

1 James Thurber and White were office mates and fellow writers at *The New Yorker*. It was White who first submitted one of Thurber's cartoon drawings for publication.

2 An early contributor to *The New Yorker*'s Reporter at Large Department. Wolcott Gibbs once said of him, "Markey has reached the point where he believes that everything that happens to him is interesting."

The New Yorker, December 19, 1937
(Also in *Fox of Peapack* and *Poems & Sketches of E. B. White*)

FASHIONS IN DOGS

An Airedale, erect beside the chauffeur of a Rolls-Royce,
Often gives you the impression he's there from choice.

In town, the Great Dane
Is kept by the insane.

Today the Boxer
Is fashionable and snappy;
But I never saw a Boxer
Who looked thoroughly happy.

The Scotty's a stoic,
He's gay and he's mad;
His pace is a snail trot,
His harness is plaid.
I once had a bitch,
Semi-invalid, crazy:
There ne'er was a Scotch girl
Quite like Daisy.

Pekes
Are biological freaks.
They have no snout
And their eyes come out.
Ladies choose 'm
To clutch to their bosom.
A Pekinese would gladly fight a wolf or a cougar
But is usually owned by a Mrs. Applegate Krueger.

Cockers are perfect for Elizabeth Barrett Browning,
Or to carry home a package from the A&P without clowning.

The wire-haired fox
Is hard on socks
With or without clocks.

The smooth-haired variety
Has practically vanished from nice society,
And it certainly does irk us
That you never see one except when you go to the circus.

The dachshund's affectionate,
He wants to wed with you:
Lie down to sleep,
And he's in bed with you.
Sit in a chair,
He's there.
Depart,
You break his heart.

My Christmas will be a whole lot wetter and merrier
If somebody sends me a six-weeks-old Boston terrier.

Sealyhams have square sterns and cute faces
Like toy dogs you see at Macy's.
But the Sealyham, while droll in appearance,
Has no clearance.

Chows come in black, and chows come in red;
They could come in bright green, I wouldn't turn my head.
The roof of their mouth is supposed to be blue,
Which is one of those things that might easily be true.

To us it has never seemed exactly pleasant
To see a beautiful setter on East Fifty-seventh Street looking
    for a woodcock or a pheasant.

German shepherds are useful for leading the blind,
And for biting burglars and Consolidated Edison men in the
    behind.

Lots of people have a rug.
Very few have a pug.

LETTER TO GLUYAS WILLIAMS

245 East 48
9 June 1938

Dear Gluyas:

We were delighted to hear that you would be going to Deer Isle after all.[1] The almost total demolition of our nice white house has pretty well taken the starch out of us, but we will soon be in residence among the ruins, and maybe we can make something of it all. Here in town we are desperately trying to wind up our affairs, dwelling in the sad residue of overstuffed furniture and underdone memories—bare floors, half empty shelves, untouched closets whose doors we dare not open. The paraphernalia of life are really appalling, when you start stirring them up. Kay left for Pomfret this morning to attend Roger's graduation; Nancy finished at Bryn Mawr last week. Joe staged his own celebration with a fever of 103, scaring the daylights out of us, but quickly subsided. In the general turbulence I find I am unable to get any work done of any sort, and spend my time trying to decide whether or not to throw away my biology notebook

(Mount Vernon High School), examining the dog for fleas, and running errands. However, the steady disappearance of beds, chairs, mirrors, rugs, drapes, glass, china, and oddments is clearing my blood; we've been holding private sales with considerable success (our prices are right) and in another ten days I hope to be without a pencil to my name, except what's in North Brooklin.

I'll probably leave by car about the 16th, taking Joe, Freddie, Ezekiel (a new puppy), Nick (a bird), Hattie (a rubber plant), and a sack of middlings. Kay will depart a couple of days later, by train, after closing the house and mopping up. (I must remember to get that girl a mop.)

My piece "Memoirs of a Master"[2] which you mentioned in your letter wasn't a brilliant success. The *Saturday Evening Post* canned it, so I retired it to stud. I am an easily discouraged fellow. See you soon.

Andy

1 For many years, *New Yorker* cartoonist and artist, Gluyas Williams, and his family had a summer home on Sylvester's Cove, Deer Isle. They and the Whites used to visit back and forth.

2 The piece was published in the December 23, 1939, *New Yorker* and later collected in *A Subtreasury of American Humor* (signed M.R.A.), edited by E. B. White and Katharine S. White.

Letter to Ik Shuman[1]

North Brooklin, Maine
[July 1938]
Sunday

Dear Ik:
As to yrs of July 14 regarding my sending some timely comment
the weeks of Aug. 27 and Sept. 3, I would say that I believe I can
do this all right. If I can't I am not the same old White. Maybe I
am not. Lying under a range shelter holding a clinching iron
against the roost supports, I sometimes wonder. You didn't say
what quantity of this comment, or "guano," you wanted. You
mean two whole departments, or what? I would like some comment suggestions to work from in the event that I undertake this
writing job. Writing is at best menial work, and I need suggestions, or the "folder."
    My black dog got a woodchuck yesterday and ate most of it.
Later he was sick.
Yrs,
Andy

1 White wrote, "Ik Shuman was the current 'Jesus' at *The New Yorker*.
Ross was always hiring someone to run the magazine and then not letting them run it."

Letter to H. K. Rigg[1]

North Brooklin, Maine
15 September 1938

Dear Bun:

I liked your S.S. *Princess Anne* very much, and think she looks like an ocarina.[2] My own Palatial Ferry has a dead engine at the moment, the base being full of water instead of cylinder oil. I haven't found out where the water comes from, but the barber-shop opinion around here is that the jacket has rusted through. Doubt very much that she was properly laid up last fall, as the boatyard man had a mad on. I am the one that has the mad on now, and am thinking of hauling her on my own beach, and letting [Alan Cole] superintend the operation. . . . *Astrid's* new mainsail has had a nice workout this summer and sets good. She also sports a new jumbo which I had cut here in Sargentville, for thirteen bucks. We had a lousy summer on the whole, with plenty of rain and all kinds of goings on, structural and otherwise. The new cellar wasn't used to her concrete floor, and proceeded to fill up with water so that we had to go after a jar of jam in hip boots. The chimneys work all right but they go through the attic at the god damnedest angle you ever saw in a chimney. I am scared of earthquakes. Right now I am shingling the barn, which is nice clean work if you don't slip. On the whole the general situation is improving—Joe has started school already, and there is no longer any low hum of guests around the place. The Eureka Pavilion ("Amusements of All Kinds")[3] is settling into its stride, roller skating on Monday and Thursday nights until further notice, coming soon Harold Lloyd in "Professor Beware." My broilers are now roasters and very good eating. One of these days I am going wild bee hunting, as one of my pals is an expert.

Ezekiel (Zeke), a black Labrador retriever, in front of the North Brooklin barn

Yesterday morning the cove was full of coots.

Zeke has turned out to be quite a dog, and is far and away the best clown on the place. He had a field day when the North East cruise was in here, cleaning up after them on the shore. For three days I never saw him when he didn't have a Lily cup or a thermos bottle in his mouth. He is very quick and big, and those young sailors, broiling their lobsters and opening their hard boiled eggs, hardly stood a chance. Right now he has a fine black coat, beautifully marked with red lead.[4] He hasn't got the amiable and noble disposition that Moses had, but is a lot gayer and brighter.

If you get tired of the 'untin' set, and can't locate another coon dog named Rock, you better drift down here and we'll catch a mackerel, or a wild bee. Kay says to tell Frances she saw her aunt Mrs. Clark at a brawl right here in Brooklin. How is everything on 49th Street, or even 48th? I am supposed to be doing a monthly department for *Harper's*; and what with a deadline of 40 days, and war trouble in Czechoslovakia, it is a tough life. I never should have got into this monthly racket.

Love to all,
Andy

1 H. K. Rigg, called "Bun" (as was one of White's brothers, Stanley), was a yacht broker who wrote a column on yachting for *The New Yorker*. He later became editor of *Skipper Magazine*.
2 An ocarina is an oval wind instrument, related to the flute.
3 The Eureka Pavillion once stood in the center of Brooklin between the library and the church.
4 Boats were painted below the waterline with red lead paint to protect the hull.

LETTER TO JAMES THURBER

North Brooklin, Maine
18 November 1938

Dear Jim:

Thanksgiving won't seem like Thanksgiving to us away from the Thurber house, but we didn't see how we could make it. It turns out Elsie [Sergeant] is coming here for a week's visit, and anyway Woodbury isn't within our weekend range, even with me at the wheel. There are something like 452 miles separating you and yours from us and ourn. I am getting to be more realistic about mileage than I used to be: even to go to the movies we must drive 28 miles there and 28 miles back. Joe goes 2.5 miles to school—partly on the hoof, partly motor-driven. Kay goes 46.6 to get her hair washed—and is lucky even at that. We go 51 miles to meet trains, 28 miles to buy a bottle of Amontillado, 9 miles to a package of Kleenex, 13.6 miles to a cord of slabwood; and even to harvest the two dozen eggs which my pullets lay daily (at no prearranged signal from me) I have to walk 100 feet. My pullets are laying fools, but they have a strange thing the matter with

Katharine Angell and James Thurber with his Scotty, Jennie (Daisy's mother);
Sneden's Landing, New York, February 1929

them which causes them to shake their heads. I have looked this up in my pamphlets, but I can't find out much. It's like a dog biting himself viciously in the pocket under his hind leg—you can't tell much about it, whether it's worms or fleas or eczema. These birds of mine never stop shaking their heads and it is beginning to get to me. Sometimes I stand there and get thinking that maybe they are shaking their heads over me. "Poor old White," they say, shaking their heads. I asked Lennie Candage what it meant when they started shaking their heads. (Lennie was over here building a new foundation wall under the north end of the barn so it wouldn't be too cold for the pig in the barn cellar: and there is a story in that, too, it's what always happens to me—I get a pig so that we won't have to buy hams, and then I rebuild my barn around the pig at an expense of perhaps a thousand hams, or more than you and I could eat (with mustard) during the rest of our natural lives, if you can call mine a natural life.) End parenthesis. Anyway, Lennie was here, his old felt hat a mass of spider webs where he'd been walking around in cellars doing foundation work, and when I put it right up to him about my pullets shaking their heads he said, "God, I dunno nuthin' 'bout chickens. I just feed 'em, and if they do good I take the money; if they sicken, I dump 'em. That's all I know 'bout chickens." Just the same, I wish they'd stop shaking their heads.[1]

On the whole we are getting along here pretty well and liking it. There is something in me that keeps making me want to do things I am not very good at, and of course the country is the ideal place for that. I have made things about as hard for myself as anybody conceivably could, I guess, what with installing a coal furnace that has to be handfired (by me), and acquiring a lot of miscellaneous live animals that have to be fed, watered, nursed, wormed, bedded, scolded, and worried about. This place teems with trouble, of one sort and another. I am up every morning at twenty past six, trouble shooting. The community here is a very strange box of bon bons, with a surprise in every layer. In summer time it is impossible to find out much about what goes on but in winter you begin to get to know people.

(Later, Sat. the 26) We had a light fall of snow for Thanksgiving Day, and yesterday we awoke to a N.E. blizzard, a gale of wind and plenty of what the sportswriter on the Bangor News calls the fine white particles. The wind was blowing so hard the snow never hit the ground at all, just went along till it brought up against something. When Kay learned that no milk had come and that the power lines were down, she was just like Mrs. Peterkin on the famous morning when the Peterkins arose to find a white world and no butcher. I spent most of the morning applying hot towels to frozen pipes in the woodshed, rescuing small animals and birds from strange unsuitable locations, stoking fires, and battening down barn doors. We soon were without water, the power being off, and this suggested a trip to the spring—which is across the road in an alder thicket, about three hundred and fifty feet away. I remembered that I had equipped the spring with a concrete cover, and that in my zeal I had fitted this cover with a large, cheap padlock—the sort of elaborate, fussy gesture which a city man makes when he first comes to the country and begins tampering with fundamental matters, like water. It is an exciting moment, when you renew your acquaintance with a spring (a locked spring) during a driving snowstorm. Joe and I and the hired man fought our way through drifts groin high, dragging our buckets. Things were a little quieter in the woods, and we scraped the snow off the spring top and Joe applied oil to the lock. I had brought a hack saw along. It seemed an odd thing to approach a pure spring of water with, a hack saw. To my surprise the lock gradually loosened up and admitted us to my water, which we scooped out in enamel pails and lugged back through the blizzard to the house. It wasn't that anybody particularly wanted any water, either. Nobody wanted any water. Six hours later the power came on again, and with it the full pipe, the pure-flowing tap.

Yesterday was the day, too, when Ethelbert ("Mighty Lak a Rose") Nevin's daughter Doris had invited us to dinner to meet Mary Ellen Chase. But not even as idyllic a literary occasion as that could take place in such a great storm: the snowplow hadn't come through, and there was just no getting authors together. We've got another storm in our lap, but are taking it quietly—we have laid down our hack saws and will beat them into plowshares come spring.

We are very lucky in our "help" this fall, our dinners being cooked for us by Miss Milly Gray, a kindly white-haired lady . . . [who] is full of prophecy and lore of all kinds. She looks under the lid of the stove for signs of milder weather. She has a humorous regard for a set of deities called "they." Her references to these spirits are always made with a half deprecatory manner, as though they were a rather troublesome, quirky, ill-tempered group of gods. "I was thinkin' one snowstorm might be enough for one week," she said this morning, "but they didn't think that way." Or, commenting on my Labrador retriever, "They didn't skimp any, when they made that one, did they?" She keeps up a running stream of conversation with herself, alone in the kitchen, and has a lively interest in wild flowers.

Life is just about alarming as it ever was, it seems to me. I worry some about my brothers and sisters, most of whom are in one sort of trouble or another. The piano business has folded, leaving Albert clean. My Washington sister [Clara Wyvell] is giving up her boarding house and going to a small town in upstate New York to live with a sister-in-law. Art Illian has moved from Chicago to Kew Gardens—which somehow sounds unpropitious. And my brother Stanley, while still teaching landscape architecture at the University of Illinois, is fooling with a patent on something called Botanical Bricks. My book of poems has brought me a handful of letters, from people like Ada Trimingham and the man I bought the touring car from. But it is apparent from reviews and sales that I will have to write something a whole lot better than that if I am to continue in this game. I don't know which is more discouraging, literature or chickens. Roup, favus, thrush, range paralysis, the spiral stomach worm, the incessant shaking of the head—these specters take their place alongside rejected newsbreaks, teeny books of poems, and the exhaustion which comes with the fortieth birthday. Incidentally, my fear of mold, which you mentioned in your piece, is still strong; and I am delighted to learn in my poultry bulletin that my birds and I may be called away together. There are several poultry diseases caused by fungi (molds), the most common being *Aspergillosis*. The causative agents are the common green mold, *Aspergillus fumigatus,* and the black mold, *A. niger,* which grow on vegetables and other kinds of matter. The affected birds mope, separate themselves from the remainder of the flock, or remain in a sitting posture. The difficulty of breathing increases rapidly; they gasp for breath and make movements of the head and neck as if choking; there are fever, diarrhea, drooping wings, great depression, a tendency to sleep, and finally suffocation and death. Thrush is another fungi trouble. In bad thrush cases, you have to flush out the crop with a 2-percent boric acid solution. I haven't yet met the chicken which would let me flush out its crop, but a man never knows.

You and Helen must pay us a call soon. It is bleak here for visitors, and uninteresting, but we expect them to come just the same. I will try to have my ice boats made by the time you arrive. An ice boat is a good way to get away from mold—except, of course, the sail. The sail gets moldy, and you have to watch it.

Lots of love, and thanks for the invitation to Thanksgiving.

Yrs,

Andy

1 It was Candage who gave White his most prized bit of agricultural advice: "The time to cut hay is in hayin' time."

LETTER TO FRANK SULLIVAN

North Brooklin, Maine
20 December 1938

Dear Frank:

I got your letter (October 19, 1938) and your clipbook[1] ("Oyster of Great Price") and will now sit down and thank you for them. It is great to be sitting down. There is not enough of that done here on my place—in fact, the turbulence of country life is a disillusioning, or at any rate, an unexpected factor in this change of residence. I had looked forward to long cozy evenings around the blazing birch fire, with my dog dozing at my feet and in my hands a good book ("How to Raise an Oyster," by Frank Sullivan) but the fact is we spend most of the 24 hours on a quick scamper and my room is clogged with unopened copies of the *New York Times*, probably full of rather nasty news. I'm up about six every morning, and immediately after breakfast I take a mild sedative to keep from getting too damn stirred up over the events of the day, the heady rhythm of earth, the intoxicating wine-dark sea which laps my pasture, the thousand and one exciting little necessities which spring from a 12-room steam-heated house standing all alone in a big world. There is a strong likelihood that the country will be my undoing, as I like it too well and take it too seriously. I have taken these 40 acres to be my bride, and of course that can be exhausting. I dance attendance on my attractive holdings, all day long. Kay and I are both drawing closer and closer to an electric water pump, farther and farther from the world of books ("With Pearls in Arabia"). I don't even have my dog dozing at my feet in the evening because we've got it figured out that if he is going to sleep in the cold barn after we go to bed, he ought not lay around in the living room getting overheated. So we put the poor bastard out right after supper, to shiver in his straw pile twelve hours instead of only eight. All kinds of odd complications like that about Maine life. This afternoon I ought to do news-breaks, but instead of that I have to make a motor trip of 54 miles to buy some tiny cardboard boxes in which the members of the Parent-Teacher Association will place the popcorn and candy for the children of Brooklin. In New York I never indulged in any charitable nonsense like that, but in this town we are at the moment the No. 1 glamour family, the family to which the leading citizens instinctively turn in any crisis. In NY I never attended a PTA meeting, figuring that a parent went through enough hell right in his own home—and besides, there was always some other place you could go, like to a professional hockey game; but I wouldn't miss the PTA meetings here. It was at the last meeting that they voted to raise the salary of the librarian in the Brooklin library. She now gets $13 a year. I believe it's to be almost doubled. They're even talking of putting lights in the library, so people can see to read after dark. (It gets dark here at ten past three in the afternoon.)

The trouble with Maine is it has too distinguished a past. Every day the *Bangor Daily News* runs a long feature piece on Maine lore or history, usually an interview with an octogenarian who still thinks of himself as returning from the China Seas with a sandalwood box for his bride—or a bride for his sandalwood box. Or he is in a clipper ship in a gale off the Horn. I think this kind of reading makes the present generation restless and unhappy, and they are always looking for something bold to do. We had a blizzard on Thanksgiving, and somebody suddenly remembered that there were a lot of deer hunters in the woods, so the state cops rounded up a squadron of snowplows (which were badly needed right where they stood) and went bursting through a woods road on a rescue expedition which would have been a lifesaver for a cliché expert dying of exposure. Giant planes roared from the Bangor airport and swooped down to drop bundles of food and first aid supplies to stormbound hunters. The Field Artillery horned in on the fun, and as near as I can make out held up the operations considerably by insisting on establishing short wave radio communication between the tractor plows and the Artillery base in Bangor. (I have often wondered what an artilleryman says to a driver of a snowplow, but apparently he has a message.) The story made great reading and got better and better, until, toward the end of the fifth column on Page 2, it turned out that quite a few of the hunters wanted to stay in the woods "until later in the week." The hunting was just getting good, and all the hunters from around here have enough rye in camp to keep them till spring anyway.

On the whole we are getting along fine, miss our friends some, but not too much; we have pork chops hanging by strings in the garage, apples in the attic, jams and thermostats in the root cellar, and a spruce tree waiting for me to chop it. I also have an instep waiting for the first merry axblow. We were tickled to get your book, and your Hollywood visit piece (which I had never read) wowed me. Would like to be in the pool with you now, treading champagne. K sends love.

Merry Christmas,

Andy

1 *A Pearl in Every Oyster.* Frank Sullivan was a fellow Cornell student and, later, a frequent contributor to *The New Yorker.*

A Boston Terrier

I would like to hand down a dissenting opinion in the case of the Camel ad that shows a Boston terrier relaxing. I can string along with cigarette manufacturers to a certain degree, but when it comes to the temperament and habits of terriers, I shall stand my ground.

The ad says: "A dog's nervous system resembles our own." I don't think a dog's nervous system resembles my own in the least. A dog's nervous system is in a class by itself. If it resembles anything at all, it resembles the Consolidated Edison Company's power plant. This is particularly true of Boston terriers, and if the Camel people don't know that, they have never been around dogs.

The ad says: "But when a dog's nerves tire, he obeys his instincts—he relaxes." This, I admit, is true. But I should like to call attention to the fact that it sometimes takes days, even weeks, before a dog's nerves tire. In the case of terriers it can run into months. I knew a Boston terrier once (he is now dead and, so far as I know, relaxed) whose nerves stayed keyed up from the twenty-fifth of one June to the sixth of the following July, without one minute's peace for anybody in the family. He was an old dog and he was blind in one eye, but his infirmities caused no diminution in his nervous power. During the period of which I speak, the famous period of his greatest excitation, he not only raised a type of general hell that startled even his closest friends and observers, but he gave a mighty clever excuse. He said it was love.

"I'm in love," he would scream. (He could scream just like a hurt child.) "I'm in love, and I'm going crazy. "

Day and night it was all the same. I tried everything to soothe him. I tried darkness, cold water dashed in the face, the lash, long quiet talks, warm milk administered internally, threats, promises, and close confinement in remote locations. At last, after about a week of it, I went down the road and had a chat with the lady who owned the object of our terrier's affection. It was she who finally cleared up the situation.

"Oh," she said, wearily, "if it's that bad, let him out."

I hadn't thought of anything as simple as that myself, but I am a creature of infinite reserve. As a matter of record, it turned out to be not so simple—the terrier got run over by a motor car one night while returning from his amorous adventures, suffering a complete paralysis of the hip but no assuagement of the nervous system, and the little Scotty bitch returned to Washington, D.C., and a Caesarian section.

I am not through with the Camel people yet. Love is not the only thing that can keep a dog's nerves in a state of perpetual jangle. A dog, more than any other creature, it seems to me, gets interested in one subject, theme, or object, in life, and pursues it with a fixity of purpose that would be inspiring to Man if it weren't so troublesome. One dog gets absorbed in one thing, another dog in another. When I was a boy there was a smooth-haired fox terrier (in those days nobody ever heard of a fox terrier that wasn't smooth-haired) who became interested, rather late in life, in a certain stone. The stone was about the size of an egg. As far as I could see, it was like a million other stones—but to him it was the Stone Supreme.

He kept it with him day and night, slept with it, ate with it, played with it, analyzed it, took it on little trips (you would often see him three blocks from home, trotting along on some shady errand, his stone safe in his jaws). He used to lie by the hour on the porch of his house, chewing the stone with an expression half tender, half petulant. When he slept he merely enjoyed a muscular suspension: his nerves were still up and around, adjusting the bed clothes, tossing and turning.

He permitted people to throw the stone for him and people would. But if the stone lodged somewhere he couldn't get to he raised such an uproar that it was absolutely necessary that the stone be returned, for the public peace. His absorption was so great it brought wrinkles to his face, and he grew old before his time. I think he used to worry that somebody was going to pitch the stone into a lake or a bog, where it would be irretrievable. He wore off every tooth in his jaw, wore them right down to the gums, and they became mere brown vestigial bumps. His breath was awful (he panted night and day) and his eyes were alight with an unearthly zeal. He died in a fight with another dog. I have always suspected it was because he tried to hold the stone in his mouth all through the battle. The Camel people will just have to take my word for it: that dog was a living denial of the whole theory of relaxation. He was a paragon of nervous tension, from the moment he first laid eyes on his slimy little stone till the hour of his death.

The advertisement speaks of the way humans "prod" themselves to endeavor—so that they keep on and on working long after they should quit. The inference is that a dog never does that. But I have a dog right now that can prod himself harder and drive himself longer than any human I ever saw. This animal is a dachshund, and I shall spare you the long dull inanities of his innumerable obsessions. His particular study (or mania) at the moment is a black-and-white kitten that my wife gave me for Christmas, thinking that what my life needed was something else that could move quickly from one place in the room to another. The dachshund began his research on Christmas Eve when the kitten arrived "secretly" in the cellar, and now, five months later, is taking his Ph.D. still working late at night on it, every night. If he could write a book about that cat, it would make *Middletown* look like the work of a backward child.

I'll be glad to have the Camel people study this animal in one of his relaxed moods, but they will have to bring their own seismograph. Even curled up cozily in a chair, dreaming of his cat, he quivers like an aspen.

LETTER TO CLARA WHITE WYVELL[1]

North Brooklin, Maine
14 Jan. [1940?]

Dear Tar:
You can bring anybody except you better not bring that cattle man, as I have sheep here and there is a continual feud between us sheep raisers and those cattle men. Let me know when you are coming and I will send you some road information that ought to be very useful to you, as I am an authority on New England highway pitfalls.

We have had a good winter so far, nobody has broken his neck, and the weather has been cold and clear. The snow we got before New Year's is still with us, although it is beginning to peter out now. It will be wonderful to see you again, as it seems to me it has been a long while. The place we live in is twenty-five miles from a movie, but I will take you every night just the same. During the daytime you can collect eggs, or you can hunt for gloves. We spend most of our time hunting for gloves, as I have a dachshund puppy who hides them on us. If you have any gloves, don't bring them, as you will never see them again.

Our guest rooms are all on the north side. Nobody lasts long in them. Don't forget to put some anti-freeze mixture in your car radiator and drink some yourself. I don't know whether you own any woolen underdrawers, because it is none of my business, but they are the only kind that do any good. I have never worn an overcoat since coming here to live. It is all done with woolen

underdrawers. Remember my warning never to visit me between the first and the tenth of any month!
EBW

1 Clara ("Tar") was White's sister, the second child in the family after Marion. She married an attorney named Manton Marble Wyvell and they had nine children, seven of whom survived.

LETTER TO JOEL WHITE

Joel was nine years old at the time of this letter.

The Grosvenor
35 Fifth Avenue
New York
[June 23, 1940]
Sunday

Dear Joe:

From my hotel window I can see the apartment building on Eighth Street where we used to live when you were a baby. I can also see the trees of Washington Square, and the backyards of the houses on Ninth Street with their little gardens of potted plants and trellises. The Sixth Avenue Elevated is gone, and New York looks very different on that account. People still like to come out in their sun-suits on Sunday morning and sun themselves in their roof gardens, and they still spend a good deal of time taking dogs out for a walk, not realizing how lucky they are that there are no porcupines. Everybody that I talk to is very gloomy about the war and about the defeat of France, but that is true everywhere today. In Radio City, where we used to skate, there is an open-air restaurant, with people sitting at little tables under big green umbrellas. The fountain is going and makes a great noise.

Joel White, about age ten, driving the hay truck with his dog, Raffles.
E. B. White purchased a 25-cent ticket and won Raffles, a wire-haired
fox terrier puppy. He brought him home in his pocket and gave him to Joel.

How has everything been going in Maine? I miss you a lot and wish I could be there right now, although my hay fever bothers me less in the city than in the country. Is Barney[1] coming to cut the hay? I hope so. And did you get any Barred Rock chicks from Mr. Sylvester?[2] Tell me all about these things, and whether you have caught any fish.

There is a church right opposite the hotel, and every afternoon the chimes ring at about five o'clock when people are coming home from work. It reminds me of being a student at Cornell, where the chimes in the library tower used to ring every afternoon toward the end of day. I suppose right now the bell in the church in Brooklin is ringing, too, five hundred miles from here.

Tell Mother that everything is going along all right, and that I'll try to get a good deal of work done in the next few days so that

I'll be able to be back in Maine soon. I'm still hoping that you and I can take a little camping trip this summer, so you better keep your ax sharpened up and your boots oiled. I hope you'll help Mother as much as you can while I'm away. Give my love to her and to everybody, and write me if you get time.

Affectionately,

Dad

1 "Barney Steele," writes White, "was a Joel White hero who had a team of workhorses and who sometimes let a boy take the reins."
2 Leon F. Sylvester, poultryman and storekeeper, of South Blue Hill.

Harper's Magazine, November 1940
"One Man's Meat" column (not in OMM book)

WARTIME DACHSHUNDS

One change which has come about since the World War is the change in people's feeling about dachshunds. I remember that in the last war if a man owned a dachshund he was suspected of being pro-German. The growth in popularity of the standard breeds has brought about a spirit of tolerance, almost a spirit of understanding. My neighbors here in the country don't seem to attach any dark significance to our dachshunds, Fred and Minnie. In this war if you own a dachshund people don't think you are pro-Nazi; they just think you are eccentric.

Dog Training

There is a book out called *Dog Training Made Easy,* and it was sent to me the other day by the publisher, who rightly guessed that it would catch my eye. I like to read books on dog training. Being the owner of dachshunds, to me a book on dog discipline becomes a volume of inspired humor. Every sentence is a riot. Some day, if I ever get a chance, I shall write a book, or warning, on the character and temperament of the Dachshund and why he can't be trained and shouldn't be. I would rather train a striped zebra to balance an Indian club than induce a dachshund to heed my slightest command. For a number of years past I have been agreeably encumbered by a very large and dissolute dachshund named Fred. Of all the dogs whom I have served I've never known one who understood so much of what I say or held it in such deep contempt. When I address Fred I never have to raise either my voice or my hopes. He even disobeys me when I instruct him in something that he wants to do. And when I answer his peremptory scratch at the door and hold the door open for him to walk through, he stops in the middle and lights a cigarette, just to hold me up.

"Shopping for a puppy presents a number of problems," writes Mr. Wm. Cary Duncan, author of *Dog Training Made Easy.* Well, shopping for a puppy has never presented many problems for me, as most of the puppies and dogs that have entered my life (and there have been scores of them) were not the result of a shopping trip but of an act of God. The first puppy I owned, when I was about nine years old, was not shopped for—it was born to the collie bitch of the postman of my older sister, who sent it to me by express from Washington, D.C., in a little crate containing, in addition to the puppy, a bar of Peters' chocolate and a ripe

Joel White training Raffles to pull a berry basket

frankfurter. And the puppy I own now was not shopped for but was won in a raffle. Between these two extremes there have been many puppies, mostly unshopped for. It is not so much that I acquire dogs as it is that dogs acquire me. Maybe they even shop for me, I don't know. If they do I assume they have many problems, because they certainly always arrive with plenty, which they then turn over to me.

The possession of a dog today is a different thing from the possession of a dog at the turn of the century, when one's dog was fed on mashed potato and brown gravy and lived in a doghouse with an arched portal. Today a dog is fed on scraped beef and Vitamin B1 and lives in bed with you.

An awful lot of nonsense has been written about dogs by persons who don't know them very well, and the attempt to elevate the purebred to a position of national elegance has been, in the main, a success. Dogs used to mate with other dogs rather casually in my day, and the results were discouraging to the American Kennel Club but entirely satisfactory to small boys who liked puppies. In my suburban town, "respectable" people didn't keep she-dogs. One's washerwoman might keep a bitch, or one's lawn cutter, but not one's next-door neighbor.

The prejudice against females made a deep impression on me, and I grew up thinking that there was something indecent and unclean about she-things in general. The word bitch of course was never used in polite families. One day a little mutt followed me home from school, and after much talk I persuaded my parents to let me keep it—at least until the owner turned up or advertised for it. It dwelt among us only one night. Next morning my father took me aside and in a low voice said: "My son, I don't know whether you realize it, but that dog is a female. It'll have to go."

"But why does it have to?" I asked.

"They're a nuisance," he replied, embarrassed. "We'd have all the other dogs in the neighborhood around here all the time."

That sounded like an idyllic arrangement to me, but I could tell from my father's voice that the stray dog was doomed. We turned her out and she went off toward the more liberal section of town. This sort of incident must have been happening to thousands of American youngsters in those days, and we grew up to find that it had been permanently added to the record by Dorothy Parker in her short story, "Mr. Durant."

On our block, in the days of my innocence, there were in addition to my collie, a pug dog, a dachshund named Bruno, a fox terrier named Sunny who spent many years studying one croquet ball, a red setter, and a St. Bernard who carried his mistress's handbag, shuffling along in stately fashion with the drool running out both sides of his jaws. I was scared of this St. Bernard because of his size, and never passed his house without dread.

The dachshund was old, surly, and disagreeable, and was endlessly burying bones in the flower border of the DeVries's yard. I should very much doubt if any of those animals ever had its temperature taken rectally, ever was fed raw meat or tomato juice, ever was given distemper inoculations, or ever saw the whites of a veterinary's eyes. They were brought up on chicken bones and gravy and left-over cereal and were all fine dogs. Most of them never saw the inside of their owner's houses—they knew their place.

The "problem" of caring for a dog has been unnecessarily complicated. Take the matter of housebreaking. In the suburbia of those lovely post-Victorian days of which I write, the question of housebreaking a puppy was met with the simple bold courage characteristic of our forefathers. You simply kept the house away from the puppy. This was not only the simplest way, it was the only practical way, just as it is today. Our parents were in possession of a vital secret—a secret which has been all but lost to the world: the knowledge that a puppy will live and thrive without ever crossing the threshold of a dwelling house, at least till he's big enough so he doesn't wet the rug.

Although our fathers and mothers very sensibly never permitted a puppy to come into the house, they made up for this indignity by calling the puppy "Sir." In those days a dog didn't expect anything very elaborate in the way of food or medical care, but he did expect to be addressed civilly.

Mr. Duncan discusses housebreaking at some length and assumes, as do all writers of dog books, that the owner of a puppy has little else to do except own the puppy. It is Mr. Duncan's theory that puppies have a sense of modesty and don't like to be stared at when they are doing something. When you are walking the dog, he says, you must "appear utterly uninterested" as you approach some favorite spot. This, as any city dweller knows, is a big order. Anybody who has ever tried to synchronize a puppy's bowels with a rigid office schedule knows that one's interest in the small phenomena of early morning sometimes reaches fever pitch. A dog owner may feign disinterest, but his mask will not suffice. Nothing is more comical than the look on the face of a person at the upper end of a dog leash, pretending not to know what is going on at the lower.

A really companionable and indispensable dog is an accident of nature. You can't get it by breeding for it, and you can't buy it with money. It just happens along. Out of the vast sea of assorted dogs that I have had dealings with, by far the noblest, the best, and the most important was the first, the one my sister sent me in a crate. He was an old-style collie, beautifully marked, with a blunt nose and great natural gentleness and intelligence. When I got him he was what I badly needed. I think probably all these other dogs of mine have been just a groping toward that old dream. I've never dared get another collie for fear the comparison would be too uncomfortable. I can still see my first dog in all the moods and mutations that memory has filed him away in, but I think of him oftenest as he used to be right after breakfast on the back porch, listlessly eating up a dish of petrified oatmeal rather than hurt my feelings. For six years he met me at the same place after school and convoyed me home—a service he thought up himself. A boy doesn't forget that sort of association. It is a monstrous trick of fate that now, settled in the country and with sheep to take care of, I am obliged to do my shepherding with the grotesque and sometimes underhanded assistance of two dachshunds and a wire-haired fox terrier.

LETTER TO KATHARINE S. WHITE

North Brooklin, Maine
[Spring 1941]
Tues morning

Dear K:

This is one of those mornings, the decibels working up to a crescendo, with many visiting boys all of them named Hawless. Dogs bark, sheep cry, domestics chatter, Howard and I stand three feet apart and yell directions at each other, the water pump and the coffee grinder run incessantly, and the young crows cry for the old life they once knew. You don't know about the crows, I guess. We have crows, now. Joe located a nest (in the tallest spruce in the county), ascended, and brought back two babies, one for himself and one for Lawrence. He immediately sat down and wrote Lawrence the triumphal news. The crows live in the woodshed, in a crow's nest. Fred knows about it.

Your letter just came, and I'll be in Ellsworth at 8:40 on Saturday. I sent off what mail there was for you yesterday, and today there seems to be nothing of any consequence. I'm keeping right after the anthology work, and so far have eliminated a lot of stuff but haven't turned up much of any value. I have out practically every bound volume in the place, and am working on them day times, and the smaller lighter books at night, when I can't hold such heavy weights. . . .

Everything is fine here and will be finer when we get you back again. My neck is gradually solidifying [from arthritis], and I look forward (but not much) to a life of looking straight ahead.

The crows have pale blue eyes.

My goodness, the boys are now cutting the lawn.

Lots of love,
Andy

HUNTING DOGS

There were two dogs with us the night we went coon hunting. One was an old hound, veteran of a thousand campaigns, who knew what we were up to and who wasted no time in idle diversions. The other was a puppy, brought along to observe and learn; to him the star-sprinkled sky and the deep dark woods and the myriad scents and the lateness of the hour and the frosty ground were intoxicating. The excitement of departure was too much for his bowels. Tied in the truck, he was purged all the way over to Winkumpaw Brook and was hollow as a rotten log before the night was well under way. This may have had something to do with what happened.

It was great hunting that night, perfect for man and beast; a fateful night for coon. The stars leaned close, and some lost their hold and fell. I was amazed at how quickly and easily the men moved through the woods in strange country, guided by hunches and a bit of lantern gleam. The woods hit back at you if you let your guard down.

We were an odd lot. A couple of the men were in coveralls—those bunny suits garage mechanics wear. One old fellow had been all stove to pieces in a car accident; another was down with a hard cold and a racking cough; another had broken two ribs the day before and had been strapped up that afternoon by a doctor. He had killed the pain with a few shots of whiskey and the spirits had evidently reminded him of coon hunting. This fellow had a terrible thirst for water all during the night and he had a way of straying off from the main party and hugging the water courses where he could kneel and drink when the need was great. We could sometimes follow the progress of his thirst in the winking of his buglight, in some faraway valley. After a bit he would rejoin us. "I'm drier'n a covered bridge," he would say disconsolately.

I felt a strong affinity for the puppy because he and I were the new ones to this strange game, and somehow it seemed to me we were sharing the same excitement and mystery of a night in the woods. I had begun to feel the excitement back in the kitchen of the farmhouse, where the hunters had gathered, dropping in and standing about against the walls of the room. The talk began right away, all the cooning lore, the tales of being lost from three in the morning until six, and the tricks a coon would play on a dog. There was a woman in the room, wife of the owner of the old dog, and she was the only one for whom the night held no special allure. She sat knitting a huge mitten. Mostly, the hunters paid no attention to her. Only one remark went her way. One of the men, observing the mitten, asked:

"Getting that man o' yours ready for winter?"

She nodded.

"I should kill him before winter if he was mine—he's no good for anything else," the fellow continued, pleasantly.

The woman raised a grudging smile to this sure-fire witticism. She plied the needles without interruption. This obviously was not the first time she had been left at home while man and dogs went about their business, and it wasn't going to be the last time either. For her, it was just one night in a long succession of nights. This was the fall and in the fall the men hunted coon. They left after sundown and returned before sunup. That was all there was to that.

The best coon country is always far away. Men are roamers, and getting a long way from home is part of the sport. Our motorcade consisted of two vehicles, a truck for the dogs and owners, and a sedan for the hangers-on, lantern-bearers, and advisory committee. The old dog jumped into place the minute he was let out of the barn; the puppy was hoisted in and tied. The two of

71

them sat on a pile of straw just behind the cab. The man with the broken ribs got into the sedan. Nobody seemed to think it was in the least bit odd that he was going coon hunting, to walk twelve or fifteen miles in rough country. He said the adhesive tape held everything O.K. and anyway, he said, the only time his chest hurt was when he breathed.

We advanced without stealth, the truck leading. The headlights of our car shone directly in the faces of the dogs. The old dog leaned back craftily against the sideboards, to steady himself against the motion. He half closed his eyes and was as quiet on the journey as a middle-aged drummer on a way train. The pup crouched uneasily and was frequently thrown. He would rare up and sniff, then crouch again, then a curve would throw him and he would lose his balance and go down. He found a hole in the sideboards and occasionally would press his nose through to sniff the air. Then the excitement would attack his bowels and he would let go all over everything—with some difficulty because of the violent motion of the truck. The old dog observed this untidiness with profound contempt.

We got away from the highway after a while and followed a rough back road up into some country I had never been into. At last we got out and let the old hound go. He went to work instantly, dropping downhill out of sight. We could hear his little bell tinkling as he ranged about in the dim valley between us and a night-struck lake. When he picked up a scent, suddenly his full round tones went through you, and the night was a gong that had been struck. The old dog knew his business. The men, waiting around, would discuss in great detail his hunting and would describe what he was doing off there, and what the coon was doing; but I doubted that they knew, and they just kept making things up the way children do. As soon as the hound barked tree, which is a slightly different sound than the sound of the running, we followed his voice and shot the coon.

Once the dog led us to an old apple tree in an almost impenetrable thicket, and when the flashlights were shined up into the topmost branches no coon was there. The owner was puzzled and embarrassed. Nothing like this had ever happened before, he said. There was a long period of consultation and speculation, all sorts of theories were advanced. The most popular was that the coon had climbed the apple tree, then crossed, squirrel-like, into the branches of a nearby hackmatack, then descended, fooling the hound. Either this was the case or the dog had made an error. Upward of an hour was spent trying every angle of this delicious contretemps.

The puppy was held in leash most of the time, but when the first coon was treed he was allowed to watch the kill. Lights from half a dozen flashlights swept the tree top and converged to make a halo, with the coon's bright little sharp face in the center of the luminous ring. Our host lethargically drew his pistol, prolonging the climax with a legitimate sense of the theater. No one spoke while he drew a bead. The shot seemed to puncture first the night, then the coon. The coon lost his grip and landed with a thud, still alive and fighting. The old hound rushed in savagely, to grab him by the throat and finish him off. It was a big bull coon; he died bravely and swiftly, and the hound worked with silent fury. Then the puppy, in leash, was allowed to advance and sniff. He was trembling in every muscle, and was all eyes and ears and nose—like a child being allowed to see something meant only for grownups. (I felt a little that way myself.) As he stretched his nose forward timidly to inhale the heady smell of warm coon the old hound, jealous, snarled and leaped. The owner jerked back. The puppy yelped in terror. Everyone laughed. It was a youngster, getting burned by life—that sort of sight. Made you laugh.

After midnight we moved into easier country about ten miles away. Here the going was better—old fields and orchards, where the little wild apples lay in thick clusters under the trees. Old stone walls ran into the woods, and now and then there would be an empty barn as a ghostly landmark. The night grew frosty and the ground underfoot was slippery with rime. The bare birches wore the stars on their fingers, and the world rolled seductively, a dark symphony of brooding groves and plains. Things had gone well, and everyone was content just to be out in the small hours, following the musical directions of a wise and busy dog.

The puppy's owner had slipped the leash and allowed his charge to range about a bit. Nobody was paying much attention to him. The pup stayed with the party mostly, and although he was aware of the long-range operations of the older dog, he seemed to know that this was out of his class; he seemed timid of the woods and tended to stay close, contenting himself with sniffing about and occasionally jumping up to kiss someone's face. We were stepping along through the woods, the old hound near at hand, when the thing happened. Suddenly the puppy (who had not made a sound up to this point) let out a loud whoop and went charging off on a tangent. Everybody stopped dead in surprise.

"What goes on here anyway?" said somebody quietly.

The old hound was as mystified as the rest of us. This was a show-off stunt apparently, this puppy trying to bark coon. Nobody could make it out. Obviously there was no coon scent or the old dog would have picked it up instantly and been at his work.

"What in *the* devil?" asked somebody.

The puppy was howling unmercifully as though possessed. He charged here and there and came back along his own track passing us at a crazy mad pace, and diving into the woods on the other side of the trail. The yelps sounded hysterical now. Again the puppy charged back. This time as he passed we could see that he had a queer look in his eye and that his movements were erratic. He would dive one way at a terrible clip, then stop and back off as though ducking an enemy, half cringing; but he kept putting up this terrible holler and commotion. Once he came straight at me. I stepped aside and he went by screaming.

"Runnin' fit," said his owner. "That's the trouble. I can tell now by the way he acts. He's took with cramps in his bowwils and he don't know anything to do 'cept run and holler. C'mon, Dusty, c'mon, boy!"

He kept calling him softly. But Dusty was in another world and the shapes were after him. It was an eerie business, this crazy dog tearing around in the dark woods, half coming at you, half running from you. Even the old dog seemed disturbed and worried, as though to say: "You see—you *will* bring a child along, after his bedtime."

The men were patient, sympathetic now.

"That's all it is, he's took with a fit."

Dusty charged into the midst of us, scattering us. He stopped, bristling, his eyes too bright, a trace of froth at his mouth. He seemed half angry, half scared and wanting comfort. "Nothing much you can do, he'll run it off," they said.

And Dusty ran it off, in the deep dark woods, big with imaginary coons and enormous jealous old hounds, alive with the beautiful smells of the wild. His evening had been too much for him; for the time being he was as crazy as a loon. Someone suggested we go home.

We started moving up toward the cars, which were two or three fields away over where you could see the elms black against the sky. The thought of home wasn't popular. A counter suggestion was made to prolong the hunting, and we separated off into two parties, one to return to the cars, the other to cut across country with the old dog and intercept the main body where a certain woods road met the highway. I walked several more miles, and for the first time began to feel cold. It was another hour before I saw Dusty again. He was all right. All he needed was to be held in somebody's arms. He was very, very sleepy. He and I were both sleepy. I think we will both remember the first night we ever went coon hunting.

The New Yorker, October 3, 1942
The Talk of the Town
Notes and Comment

ABERCROMBIE'S DOG CATALOGUE

Abercrombie's dog catalogue came this morning, and we went to work at once to figure out what it costs to set up a medium-sized city animal in the style to which it will soon get accustomed. We did this because a friend of ours (a working girl) is considering taking a terrier into her life and she let drop the curiously innocent remark that although the dog might be a care, "of course it wouldn't hardly cost anything." For her benefit we have prepared the following rough estimate, totting up to around seventy dollars:

FURNISHINGS

Collar	1.50
Lead	3.00
Name plate	1.00
Blackout collar-radium studs	3.50
Bed—fleaproof cushion	6.00
Travelling case	18.50
Earthen bowl marked "DOG"	2.50

CLOTHES

Reefer	3.50
Raincoat	2.00

PERSONAL KIT

Comb	1.00

Brush	2.00
Tooth scraper (removes tartar)	2.00
Stripper	1.00
Extra blades (for stripper)	.50
Nail file	1.00
Nail clipper	2.25
REMEDIES, SOAPS, ETC.	
Irradiated yeast	.85
Liquo-garlic	1.00
Flea powder	1.25
Repellent (for sofa)	1.25
Bubble shampoo	1.00
Dip	.65
Eye drops	.60
Ear drops (anti-mite)	.60
Worm tablets	.60
Tonic (restores tone)	.60
INCIDENTALS	
Electric lamp (infra-red)	7.50
Shepherd whistle	1.25
Leather bone	.35
	68.75

The above, mind you, is just to set the dog up in housekeeping
and does not include luxuries, such as a tail shield (for protecting
tails that have been injured by knocking against the sides of kennels) or cedar shavings or a turtle-neck sweater. Maintenance
costs are something else again—food, doctor's bills, amusements.

A Week in November

Sunday. Arose at six, twenty-seven hours ahead of the arrival of the Sunday paper, which gets here at nine o'clock Monday morning—a very great advantage, to my way of thinking. Sunday is my busiest day, since I am without help, and I should not be able to get through it at all if there were any newspapers that had to be read.

The wind blew from the SE and brought rain and the dreariest landscape of the fall. For several hours after arising everything went wrong; it was one of those days when inanimate objects deliberately plot to destroy a man, lying in wait for him cleverly ambushed, and when dumb animals form a clique to disturb the existing order. This is the real farm bloc, this occasional conspiracy—a cow with a bruised teat, a weanling lamb lamenting her separation from the flock, a chain-stitch on a grain sack that refuses to start in the darkness, an absentee cook, a child with a fever, a fire that fails to pick up, a separator in need of a new ring, a lantern dry of kerosene, all conniving under gray skies and with the wind and rain drawing in through the windows on the south side, wetting the litter in the hen pens and causing the flame of life to sputter on the wick. I used to find my spirits sagging during intervals of this sort, but now I have learned about them and know them for what they are—a minority report. I'm not fooled any more by an ill wind and a light that fails. My memory is too good.

More and more people and families are leaving here and going up to the cities, to go into factories or into the Services. It is sad to see so many shut houses along the road. One of our former neighbors, now working in a shipyard, turned up after dinner to call for the five bushels of potatoes he had spoken for earlier in the season. He had driven here on his Sunday off to look after his affairs, including the potatoes, and he told me about the pleasures of building destroyers. We went down cellar and I got some bags and a bushel basket and we measured out the spuds while he held forth about his job. Afterward he said he had something to show me, so we went out to where his car stood and he pointed to the four brand-new tires—a man apart, not like ordinary mortals.

Tomorrow the hunting season opens and the men in these parts will put aside whatever they are doing and go into the woods after some wild meat.

Monday. Noticed this evening how gray Fred is becoming, our elderly dachshund. His trunk and legs are still red but his muzzle, after dozens of major operations for the removal of porcupine quills, is now a sort of strawberry roan, with many white hairs, the result of worry. Next to myself he is the greatest worrier and schemer on the premises and always has too many things on his mind. He not only handles all his own matters but he has a follow-up system by which he checks on all of mine to see that everything is taken care of. His interest in every phase of farming remains undiminished, as does mine, but his passion for details is a kind of obsession and seems to me unhealthy. He wants to be present in a managerial capacity at every event, no matter how trifling or routine; it makes no difference whether I am dipping a sheep or simply taking a bath myself. He is a fire buff whose blaze is anything at all. In damp weather his arthritis makes stair-climbing a tortuous and painful accomplishment, yet he groans his way down cellar with me to pack eggs and to investigate for the thousandth time the changeless crypt where the egg crates live. Here he awaits the fall of an egg to the floor and the sensual delight of licking it up—which he does with lips drawn slightly back as though in distaste at the strange consistency of the white. His hopes run always to accidents and misfortunes: the broken egg, the spilt milk, the wounded goose, the fallen lamb, the fallen cake. He also has an insane passion for a kicked football and a Roman candle, either of which can throw him into a running fit from which he emerges exhausted and frothing at the mouth. He can block a kick, or he can drop back and receive one full on the nose and run it back ten or twelve yards. His activities and his character constitute an almost uninterrupted annoyance to me, yet he is such an engaging old fool that I am quite attached to him, in a half-regretful way. Life without him would be heaven, but I am afraid it is not what I want.

This morning early, after I had milked and separated, I managed to lose my grip on the bowl of new cream as I was removing it from under the spout and lost the whole mess on the floor where it spread like lava to the corners of the room. For a moment my grief at this enormous mishap suffused my whole body, but the familiar assistance of Fred, who had supervised the separation and taken charge of the emergency, came to my relief. He cleaned up a pint and a half of cream so that you would not know that anything had happened. As charboy and scavenger he is the best dog I ever was associated with; nothing even faintly edible ever has to be cleaned up from the floor. He handles it. I allow him to eat any substance he chooses, in order to keep him in fighting trim, and I must say he has never failed me. He hasn't had a sick day either since the afternoon I salvaged him from a show window on Madison Avenue, suffering from intestinal disorders of a spectacular sort. I have since that time put out a lot of money on him, but it has all been for anaesthetics to keep him quiet during the extraction of quills. Not one cent for panaceas.

The production records being made and broken all the time by war industries have set me to work figuring out how things are going in my own plant. Tonight, after a short struggle, I computed that an egg is laid on this place every 4.2 minutes during the day. This is a great gain over three years ago when sometimes a whole hour would go by on this farm without anything of any consequence happening. I am devoting practically half my time now to producing food, food being something I can contribute to the general cause. My production goals for 1942–1943 are 100 pounds of wool, 14 lambs, 4,000 dozen eggs, 10 spring pigs, 150 pounds of broilers and roasters, 9,000 pounds of milk, and all the vegetables, berries, and fruit needed for home consumption and canning. This is not much for a full-scale farmer, but it is about right for a half-time worker when labor is precarious and implements and materials are hard to get.

Tuesday. There are two distinct wars being fought in the world. One is the actual war, bloody and terrible and cruel, a war of ups and downs. The other is the imaginary war that is the personal responsibility of the advertising men of America—the war you see pictures of in the full-page ads in the magazines. This second war is a lovely thing. We are always winning it, and the paint job stays bright on the bombers that gleam in the strong clean light of a copywriter's superlative adventure. It is a war in which only the brave and true take part, in which the great heart of America beats in clipped sentences. Every morning the ad men strap on their armor and gird for the fray, usually in four colors. We leap rivers with Goodyear and the Engineers, span oceans with Kelvinator and the Air Force, peel off from a fighter formation with the manufacturer of a snap fastener, blow the daylights out of a Jap cruiser with a lens company located in the Squibb building. The truth is of course that these manufacturers are indeed participating in mighty events because of the conversion of their plants, and every ad writer becomes a combatant by extension. Almost all of them call Hitler by his first name and taunt him openly. They identify themselves with the physical struggle and the heroic life, so that when the bomb door opens and the hand presses the lever you are never quite certain what is coming out—

a bomb or a bottle of cleaning fluid. This vicarious ecstasy of the ad men always makes me think of the hero of James Thurber's story called "The Secret Life of Walter Mitty."

Wednesday. My cow turned out to be a very large one. The first time I led her out I felt the way I did the first time I ever took a girl to the theater—embarrassed but elated. In both instances the female walked with a firmer step than mine, seemed rather in charge of the affair, and excited me with her sweet scent.

We are having a mild fall. Still no furnace fire, except an occasional slabwood blaze in the morning to take the chill off. Broccoli and chard in the garden, and of course kale, which the frost improves. I like kale: it is the nearest I come to eating grass. Even after the snow comes we still eat kale, pawing for it like a deer looking for frozen apples.

Thursday. In time, ownership of property will probably carry with it certain obligations, over and above the obligation to pay the tax and keep the mortgage going. There are signs that this is coming, and I think it should come. Today, if a landowner feels the urge, he can put a backhoe into his hillside pasture and disembowel it. He can set his plow against the contours and let his wealth run down into the brook and into the sea. He can sell his topsoil off by the load and make a gravel pit of a hayfield. For all the interference he will get from the community, he can dig through to China, exploiting as he goes. With an ax in his hand he can annihilate the woods, leaving brush piles and stumps. He can build any sort of building he chooses on his land in the shape of a square or an octagon or a milk bottle. Except in zoned areas he can erect any sort of sign. Nobody can tell him where to head in— it is his land and this is a free country. Yet people are beginning to suspect that the greatest freedom is not achieved by sheer irresponsibility. The earth is common ground and we are all overlords, whether we hold title or not; gradually the idea is taking form that the land must be held in safekeeping, that one generation is to some extent responsible to the next, and that it is contrary to the public good to allow an individual, merely because of his whims or his ambitions, to destroy almost beyond repair any part of the soil or the water or even the view.

After some years in the country, during which time I have experienced the satisfactions of working the land, building the soil, and making brown into green, I am beginning to believe that our new world that will open up after the war should be constructed round a repopulated rural America, so that a reasonably large proportion of the population shall participate in the culture of the earth. The trend is often in the opposite direction, even in peace. As things are now in America, country living is possible only for those who have either the talents and instincts of a true farmer or the means to live wherever they choose. I think there are large numbers of people who have not quite got either but who would like to (and probably should) dwell in the open and participate to some degree in the agricultural life. Good roads and electric power make the farm a likely unit for a better world, and the country should be inhabited very largely and broadly by all the people who feel at home there, because of its gift of light and air and food and security, and because it supplies a man directly, instead of indirectly. The trend toward the ownership of land by fewer and fewer individuals is, it seems to me, a disastrous thing. For when too large a proportion of the populace is supporting itself by the indirections of trade and business and commerce and art and the million schemes of men in cities, then the complexity of society is likely to become so great as to destroy its equilibrium, and it will always be out of balance in some way. But if a considerable portion of the people are occupied wholly or partially in labors that directly supply them with many things that they want, or think they want, whether it be a sweet pea or a sour pickle, then the public poise will be a good deal harder to upset.

Friday. Four hours at the spotting post today in company with my wife, who hears four-motored bombers in running brooks; but the weather was bad and we saw no planes, friendly or hostile. The post has been moved from behind the postmistress's barn to the abandoned schoolhouse across the road—not such a good view as the old post but a fine place to get work done between watches, excellent desk facilities (a choice of thirteen little desks), also a Seth Thomas clock, a good stove, an American flag, a picture of Lincoln, a backhouse, and an ancient love message carved in the entry, celebrating MYRTLE.

Saturday. Sent my trousers off for their quarterly pressing yesterday. They travel forty-nine miles to the ironing board, a round trip for them of ninety-eight miles. My pants are without question the best traveled part of me nowadays, and I sometimes envy them their excursions to town. Quite a lark, these days, to go all that distance on rubber. I noticed that the truck that called for them was driven by a girl, taking the place of the young fellow who has gone off to war. She told us that she loved the work—made her feel that she was having her part in the war effort; which surprised me, that anyone should derive that feeling from carting my pants around the country. But I feel exactly the same way about the eggs I produce, even though I know well enough that most of them are being gobbled by voracious people in the environs of Boston.

Found my wife and son and dachshund, all three, sitting under a lap robe on the back porch in the beautiful sunlight this afternoon listening to the Cornell–Yale game on a portable radio, this being the first time in two weeks my boy had been out of bed and the first time the dog had attended a Cornell game. (He was shaking like a leaf with pent-up emotion, and Cornell was behind.) But the three of them looked very wonderful and comical sitting there in their private bowl, and I laughed out loud. My wife, who is just getting through reading the autumn crop of children's books, informed me that we have a new ritual to look forward to on Christmas eve. (This was from a book called *Happy Times in Norway*.) We are to go to the barn and give an extra feeding to the animals, saying: "Eat and drink, my good cow, our Lord is born tonight." I intend to do it, and luckily I have the hay to spare this year. To make it a truly American ritual, however, I suspect we should have to wear smocks and dirndls and perhaps invite a photographer or two from *Vogue*.

LETTER TO STANLEY HART WHITE[1]

North Brooklin, Maine
Friday, Sept. 1 [1944]

Dear Stan:
I had just gone out when you phoned last night, and Aunt Caroline took the call. She is slightly deaf, and probably had to make up all the answers. The reason nobody else was in the house was that we were all out returning a visiting pig to its owner. When the owner came along the road to meet us, he looked accusingly at the pig and said: "Hell, everything I own is adrift tonight."

We are darn glad you are coming. I wrote you yesterday, pointing out that the railroad might offer you an easier journey. I am a firm believer in the rails. They lie solid and purposeful, and they cut right through the country as though they owned it. I am a great rail man—do not like planes or buses but am fond of the cars. In fact, I am hoping this fall to ride on a railroad I have always intended to try—the Belfast and Moosehead, so called because it starts at Belfast and doesn't go anywhere near Moosehead. The whole run is only forty miles, from the beginning of the line to the end, which is just a nice distance. One of the cars, I am told, has had its seats removed and kitchen chairs installed, as more practical. I will show you the timetable when you are here.

Evelyn leaves for Boston tomorrow, to go job hunting, so there is no problem about a bed. Her St. Bernard left last week, and the departure of a St. Bernard from a home is one of the finest things that can happen to the home. . . .[2] I imagine you will be here in time to dig a few potatoes. We always start digging potatoes right after Labor Day around here. The hired man does the digging, and the rest of us sit around and talk about it, sometimes picking up a spud or two and looking for rot or sunburn or net necrosis. There is a nice view of the bay from the potato patch.

Unless I hear from you to the contrary, I will meet your bus in Ellsworth on Wednesday night. If you decide on a different system for getting here, you better send me a wire.

Yrs,

En

P.S. (Sunday) Have just discovered this beautiful letter, written two days ago, under a pile of beautiful junk on my desk. Yet I seem to recall addressing an envelope to you and putting it in the mail bag. Now I wonder what was in that?

1 Stanley, sometimes called "Bun" or "Bunny," was White's next older brother, the fourth in the line of six. In order of appearance, they were Marion, Clara, Albert, Stanley, Lillian, and then Elwyn Brooks White. Of them all, White spent the most time with Stan, who was a natural teacher. Stan taught White (often called "En" within the family) how to read.

2 After Katharine's son Roger Angell was transferred to Hickam Field, in Hawaii, his wife Evelyn spent several weeks with the Whites in Maine with her dog Chloe—according to White, an insane St. Bernard who had running fits, and who insisted on rescuing swimmers who were not in need of rescue.

LETTER TO STANLEY HART WHITE

North Brooklin, Maine
12 September [1946]

Dear Bun:

I have done no work and written no letters this summer, and it has felt pretty good—except that I kept doing a lot of other equally nerve-bouncing things, such as deciding whether Joe could or couldn't take the car out each evening. (The State of Maine lets 15-year-olds have driver's licenses, probably on the theory that the younger they are the softer their bones.) It is hard on the parents, who sit home in a brittle condition hoping that the oil reserves of earth will soon peter out. The summer reached a sort of peak the day we went to the Blue Hill Fair and K tried to take a leak in the bushes just as the trap-shoot started. She came out with only a minor flesh wound, but she might as well have been through Anzio. We all thought it was very comical, and one shooter (I heard later) got 25 pigeons out of a possible 25.

The next night Joe took a thirteen-year-old girl to the Fair, and she got sick on the swings, vomiting with centrifugal force.

We are starting for Boston tomorrow morning early, to attend a wedding in Louisburg Square and to put Joe back in school. It always amazes me that the idea of weddings has persisted the way it has. Considering the amount of disturbance and trouble a wedding causes, as well as the expense and the danger of everybody getting poisoned on chicken salad that has been eked out by adding five pounds of bad veal, you wonder anybody has the guts to stage it. I think weddings would die in no time at all, if it weren't for women, who seem to get some inner (and probably shabby) excitement out of the occasion.

Boston

14 September

We got into a taxicab on Charles Street a few minutes ago, and discovered that it was driven by a grey-haired woman and a dog. The woman shifted and made change and the dog steered. Boston is perennially surprising and enjoyable. Mayor Curley's name is part of a flower arrangement in the Public Garden—welcoming the Veterans of Foreign Wars. And the ducks still follow the swan boat around the lake, picking up a living from the first class passengers.

K and I are planning to go back to Maine for a couple of weeks and then to New York for the winter. We have taken an apartment at 229 E. 48 Street. I have a book coming out this fall called "The Wild Flag"—a collection of *New Yorker* paragraphs on tremendous themes. In it I make my debut as a THINKER, which in these days is like stepping up on the guillotine platform wearing a faint smile.

Our health is neither very good nor very bad. I was delighted to learn that you had a good trip to the West. News of the family has been rather sparse this summer, but I'll be seeing some of them soon I hope.

Best to Blanche & Janice,

En

The New Yorker, February 22, 1947
Turtle Bay Diary

Dog Show Obedience Contest

Friday, 14 February. Last night to Madison Square Garden to watch the obedience contest in the Dog Show, and it resulted in a 15–0 victory for obedience, the Boston terrier abstaining. It did not seem to me, though, that this dog's abstention indicated a lack of cooperation or even a contempt for obedience but simply that the Boston terrier's mind was on other matters—which, from my own experience, is where a Boston terrier's mind is more than ninety per cent of the time. The Dog Show is the only place I know of where you can watch a lady go down on her knees in public to show off the good points of a dog, thus obliterating her own.

Essays of E. B. White
Autumn 1947
(Previously in *Second Tree from the Corner*)

Death of a Pig

I spent several days and nights in mid-September with an ailing pig and I feel driven to account for this stretch of time, more particularly since the pig died at last, and I lived, and things might easily have gone the other way round and none left to do the accounting. Even now, so close to the event, I cannot recall the hours sharply and am not ready to say whether death came on the third night or the fourth night. This uncertainty afflicts me with a sense of personal deterioration; if I were in decent health I would know how many nights I had sat up with a pig.

The scheme of buying a spring pig in blossomtime, feeding it through summer and fall, and butchering it when the solid cold weather arrives is a familiar scheme to me and follows an antique pattern. It is a tragedy enacted on most farms with perfect fidelity to the original script. The murder, being premeditated, is in the first degree but is quick and skillful, and the smoked bacon and ham provide a ceremonial ending whose fitness is seldom questioned.

Once in a while something slips—one of the actors goes up in his lines and the whole performance stumbles and halts. My pig simply failed to show up for a meal. The alarm spread rapidly. The classic outline of the tragedy was lost. I found myself cast suddenly in the role of pig's friend and physician—a farcical character with an enema bag for a prop. I had a presentiment, the very first afternoon, that the play would never regain its balance and that my sympathies were now wholly with the pig. This was slapstick—the sort of dramatic treatment that instantly appealed to my old dachshund, Fred, who joined the vigil, held the bag, and, when all was over, presided at the interment. When we slid the body into the grave, we both were shaken to the core. The loss we felt was not the loss of ham but the loss of pig. He had evidently become precious to me, not that he represented a distant nourishment in a hungry time, but that he had suffered in a suffering world. But I'm running ahead of my story and shall have to go back.

My pigpen is at the bottom of an old orchard below the house. The pigs I have raised have lived in a faded building that once was an icehouse. There is a pleasant yard to move about in, shaded by an apple tree that overhangs the low rail fence. A pig couldn't ask for anything better—or none has, at any rate. The sawdust in the icehouse makes a comfortable bottom in which to root, and a warm bed. This sawdust, however, came under suspicion when the pig took sick. One of my neighbors said he thought the pig would have done better on new ground—the same principle that applies in planting potatoes. He said there might be something unhealthy about that sawdust, that he never thought well of sawdust.

It was about four o'clock in the afternoon when I first noticed that there was something wrong with the pig. He failed to appear at the trough for his supper, and when a pig (or a child) refuses supper a chill wave of fear runs through any household, or ice-household. After examining my pig, who was stretched out in the sawdust inside the building, I went to the phone and cranked it four times. Mr. Dameron answered. "What's good for a sick pig?" I asked. (There is never any identification needed on a country phone; the person on the other end knows who is talking by the sound of the voice and by the character of the question.)

"I don't know, I never had a sick pig," said Mr. Dameron, "but I can find out quick enough. You hang up and I'll call Henry."

Mr. Dameron was back on the line again in five minutes. "Henry says roll him over on his back and give him two ounces of castor oil or sweet oil, and if that doesn't do the trick give him an injection of soapy water. He says he's almost sure the pig's plugged up, and even if he's wrong, it can't do any harm."

I thanked Mr. Dameron. I didn't go right down to the pig, though. I sank into a chair and sat still for a few minutes to think about my troubles, and then I got up and went to the barn, catching up on some odds and ends that needed tending to. Unconsciously I held off, for an hour, the deed by which I would officially recognize the collapse of the performance of raising a pig; I wanted no interruption in the regularity of feeding, the steadiness of growth, the even succession of days. I wanted no interruption, wanted no oil, no deviation. I just wanted to keep on raising a pig, full meal after full meal, spring into summer into fall. I didn't even know whether there were two ounces of castor oil on the place.

Shortly after five o'clock I remembered that we had been invited out to dinner that night and realized that if I were to dose a pig there was no time to lose. The dinner date seemed a familiar conflict: I move in a desultory society and often a week or two will roll by without my going to anybody's house to dinner or anyone's coming to mine, but when an occasion does arise, and I am summoned, something usually turns up (an hour or two in advance) to make all human intercourse seem vastly inappropriate. I have come to believe that there is in hostesses a special power of divination, and that they deliberately arrange dinners to coincide with pig failure or some other sort of failure. At any rate, it was after five o'clock and I knew I could put off no longer the evil hour.

When my son and I arrived at the pigyard, armed with a small bottle of castor oil and a length of clothesline, the pig had emerged from his house and was standing in the middle of his yard, listlessly. He gave us a slim greeting. I could see that he felt uncomfortable and uncertain. I had brought the clothesline thinking I'd have to tie him (the pig weighed more than a hundred pounds) but we never used it. My son reached down, grabbed both front legs, upset him quickly, and when he opened his mouth to scream I turned the oil into his throat—a pink, corrugated area I had never seen before. I had just time to read the label while the neck of the bottle was in his mouth. It said Puretest. The screams, slightly muffled by oil, were pitched in the hysterically high range of pig-sound, as though torture were being carried out, but they didn't last long: it was all over rather suddenly, and, his legs released, the pig righted himself.

In the upset position the corners of his mouth had been turned down, giving him a frowning expression. Back on his feet again, he regained the set smile that a pig wears even in sickness. He stood his ground, sucking slightly at the residue of oil; a few drops leaked out of his lips while his wicked eyes, shaded by their coy little lashes, turned on me in disgust and hatred. I scratched him gently with oily fingers and he remained quiet, as though trying to recall the satisfaction of being scratched when in health, and seeming to rehearse in his mind the indignity to which he had just been subjected. I noticed, as I stood there, four or five small dark spots on his back near the tail end, reddish brown in color, each about the size of a housefly. I could not make out what they were. They did not look troublesome but at the same time they did not look like mere surface bruises or chafe marks. Rather they seemed blemishes of internal origin. His stiff white bristles almost completely hid them and I had to part the bristles with my fingers to get a good look.

Several hours later, a few minutes before midnight, having dined well and at someone else's expense, I returned to the pig-house with a flashlight. The patient was asleep. Kneeling, I felt his ears (as you might put your hand on the forehead of a child) and they seemed cool, and then with the light made a careful examination of the yard and the house for sign that the oil had worked. I found none and went to bed.

We had been having an unseasonable spell of weather—hot, close days, with the fog shutting in every night, scaling for a few hours in midday, then creeping back again at dark, drifting in first over the trees on the point, then suddenly blowing across the fields, blotting out the world and taking possession of houses, men, and animals. Everyone kept hoping for a break, but the break failed to come. Next day was another hot one. I visited the pig before breakfast and tried to tempt him with a little milk in his trough. He just stared at it, while I made a sucking sound through my teeth to remind him of past pleasures of the feast. With very small, timid pigs, weanlings, this ruse is often quite successful and will encourage them to eat; but with a large, sick pig the ruse is senseless and the sound I made must have made him feel, if anything, more miserable. He not only did not crave food, he felt a positive revulsion to it. I found a place under the apple tree where he had vomited in the night.

At this point, although a depression had settled over me, I didn't suppose that I was going to lose my pig. From the lustiness of a healthy pig a man derives a feeling of personal lustiness; the stuff that goes into the trough and is received with such enthusiasm is an earnest of some later feast of his own, and when this suddenly comes to an end and the food lies stale and untouched, souring in the sun, the pig's imbalance becomes the man's, vicariously, and life seems insecure, displaced, transitory.

As my own spirits declined, along with the pig's, the spirits of my vile old dachshund rose. The frequency of our trips down the footpath through the orchard to the pigyard delighted him, although he suffers greatly from arthritis, moves with difficulty, and would be bedridden if he could find anyone willing to serve him meals on a tray.

He never missed a chance to visit the pig with me, and he made many professional calls on his own. You could see him down there at all hours, his white face parting the grass along the fence as he wobbled and stumbled about, his stethoscope dangling—a happy quack, writing his villainous prescriptions and grinning his corrosive grin. When the enema bag appeared, and the bucket of warm suds, his happiness was complete, and he managed to squeeze his enormous body between the two lowest rails of the yard and then assumed full charge of the irrigation. Once, when I lowered the bag to check the flow, he reached in and hurriedly drank a few mouthfuls of the suds to test their potency. I have noticed that Fred will feverishly consume any substance that is associated with trouble—the bitter flavor is to his liking. When the bag was above reach, he concentrated on the pig and was everywhere at once, a tower of strength and inconvenience. The pig, curiously enough, stood rather quietly through this colonic carnival, and the enema, though ineffective, was not as difficult as I had anticipated.

I discovered, though, that once having given a pig an enema there is no turning back, no chance of resuming one of life's more stereotyped roles. The pig's lot and mine were inextricably bound now, as though the rubber tube were the silver cord. From then until the time of his death I held the pig steadily in the bowl of my mind; the task of trying to deliver him from his misery became a strong obsession. His suffering soon became the embodiment of all earthly wretchedness. Along toward the end of the afternoon, defeated in physicking, I phoned the veterinary twenty miles away and placed the case formally in his hands. He was full of questions, and when I casually mentioned the dark spots on the pig's back, his voice changed its tone.

"I don't want to scare you," he said, "but when there are spots, erysipelas has to be considered."

Together we considered erysipelas, with frequent interruptions from the telephone operator, who wasn't sure the connection had been established.

"If a pig has erysipelas can he give it to a person?" I asked.

"Yes, he can," replied the vet.

"Have they answered?" asked the operator.

"Yes, they have," I said. Then I addressed the vet again. "You better come over here and examine this pig right away."

"I can't come myself," said the vet, "but McFarland can come this evening if that's all right. Mac knows more about pigs than I do anyway. You needn't worry too much about the spots. To indicate erysipelas they would have to be deep hemorrhagic infarcts."

"Deep hemorrhagic what?" I asked.

"Infarcts," said the vet.

"Have they answered?" asked the operator.

"Well," I said, "I don't know what you'd call these spots, except they're about the size of a housefly. If the pig has erysipelas I guess I have it, too, by this time, because we've been very close lately."

"McFarland will be over," said the vet.

I hung up. My throat felt dry and I went to the cupboard and got a bottle of whiskey. Deep hemorrhagic infarcts—the phrase began fastening its hooks in my head. I had assumed that there could be nothing much wrong with a pig during the months it was being groomed for murder; my confidence in the essential health and endurance of pigs had been strong and deep, particularly in the health of pigs that belonged to me and that were part of my proud scheme. The awakening had been violent and I minded it all the more because I knew that what could be true of my pig could be true also of the rest of my tidy world. I tried to put this distasteful idea from me, but it kept recurring. I took a short drink of the whiskey and then, although I wanted to go down to the yard and look for fresh signs, I was scared to. I was certain I had erysipelas.

It was long after dark and the supper dishes had been put away when a car drove in and McFarland got out. He had a girl with him. I could just make her out in the darkness—she seemed young and pretty. "This is Miss Owen," he said. "We've been having a picnic supper on the shore, that's why I'm late."

McFarland stood in the driveway and stripped off his jacket, then his shirt. His stocky arms and capable hands showed up in my flashlight's gleam as I helped him find his coverall and get zipped up. The rear seat of his car contained an astonishing amount of paraphernalia, which he soon overhauled, selecting a chain, a syringe, a bottle of oil, a rubber tube, and some other things I couldn't identify. Miss Owen said she'd go along with us and see the pig. I led the way down the warm slope of the orchard, my light picking out the path for them, and we all three climbed the fence, entered the pighouse, and squatted by the pig while McFarland took a rectal reading. My flashlight picked up the glitter of an engagement ring on the girl's hand.

"No elevation," said McFarland, twisting the thermometer in the light. "You needn't worry about erysipelas." He ran his hand slowly over the pig's stomach and at one point the pig cried out in pain.

"Poor piggledy-wiggledy!" said Miss Owen.

The treatment I had been giving the pig for two days was then repeated, somewhat more expertly, by the doctor, Miss Owen and I handing him things as he needed them—holding the chain that he had looped around the pig's upper jaw, holding the syringe, holding the bottle stopper, the end of the tube, all of us working in darkness and in comfort, working with the instinctive teamwork induced by emergency conditions, the pig unprotesting, the house shadowy, protecting, intimate. I went to bed tired but with a feeling of relief that I had turned over part of the responsibility of the case to a licensed doctor. I was beginning to think, though, that the pig was not going to live.

He died twenty-four hours later, or it might have been forty-eight—there is a blur in time here, and I may have lost or picked up a day in the telling and the pig one in the dying. At intervals during the last day I took cool fresh water down to him and at such times as he found the strength to get to his feet he would stand with head in the pail and snuffle his snout around. He drank a few sips but no more; yet it seemed to comfort him to dip his nose in water and bobble it about, sucking in and blowing out through his teeth. Much of the time, now, he lay indoors half buried in sawdust. Once, near the last, while I was attending him I saw him try to make a bed for himself but he lacked the strength, and when he set his snout into the dust he was unable to plow even the little furrow he needed to lie down in.

He came out of the house to die. When I went down, before going to bed, he lay stretched in the yard a few feet from the door. I knelt, saw that he was dead, and left him there: his face had a mild look, expressive neither of deep peace nor of deep suffering, although I think he had suffered a good deal. I went back up to the house and to bed, and cried internally—deep hemorrhagic intears. I didn't wake till nearly eight the next morning, and when I looked out the open window the grave was already being dug, down beyond the dump under a wild apple. I could hear the spade strike against the small rocks that blocked the way. Never send to know for whom the grave is dug, I said to myself, it's dug for thee. Fred, I well knew, was supervising the work of digging, so I ate breakfast slowly.

It was a Saturday morning, The thicket in which I found the gravediggers at work was dark and warm, the sky overcast. Here, among alders and young hackmatacks, at the foot of the apple tree, Lennie had dug a beautiful hole, five feet long, three feet wide, three feet deep. He was standing in it, removing the last spadefuls of earth while Fred patrolled the brink in simple but impressive circles, disturbing the loose earth of the mound so that it trickled back in. There had been no rain in weeks and the soil, even three feet down, was dry and powdery. As I stood and stared, an enormous earthworm which had been partially exposed by the spade at the bottom dug itself deeper and made a slow withdrawal, seeking even remoter moistures at even lonelier depths. And just as Lennie stepped out and rested his spade against the tree and lit a cigarette, a small green apple separated itself from a branch overhead and fell into the hole. Everything about this last scene seemed overwritten—the dismal sky, the shabby woods, the imminence of rain, the worm (legendary bed-fellow of the dead), the apple (conventional garnish of a pig).

But even so, there was a directness and dispatch about animal burial, I thought, that made it a more decent affair than human burial: there was no stopover in the undertaker's foul parlor, no wreath nor spray; and when we hitched a line to the pig's hind legs and dragged him swiftly from his yard, throwing our weight into the harness and leaving a wake of crushed grass and smoothed rubble over the dump, ours was a businesslike procession, with Fred, the dishonorable pallbearer, staggering along in the rear, his perverse bereavement showing in every seam in his face; and the post-mortem performed handily and swiftly right at the edge of the grave, so that the inwards that had caused the pig's death preceded him into the ground and he lay at last resting squarely on the cause of his own undoing.

I threw in the first shovelful, and then we worked rapidly and without talk, until the job was complete. I picked up the rope, made it fast to Fred's collar (he is a notorious ghoul), and we all three filed back up the path to the house, Fred bringing up the rear and holding back every inch of the way, feigning unusual stiffness. I noticed that although he weighed far less than the pig, he was harder to drag, being possessed of the vital spark.

The news of the death of my pig traveled fast and far, and I received many expressions of sympathy from friends and neighbors, for no one took the event lightly and the premature expiration of a pig is, I soon discovered, a departure which the community marks solemnly on its calendar, a sorrow in which it feels fully involved. I have written this account in penitence and in grief, as a man who failed to raise his pig, and to explain my deviation from the classic course of so many raised pigs. The grave in the woods is unmarked, but Fred can direct the mourner to it unerringly and with immense good will, and I know he and I shall often revisit it, singly and together, in seasons of reflection and despair, on flagless memorial days of our own choosing.

THE LIBERAL VIEW

It is perhaps worth recording the different ways the candidates groom themselves for a Presidential race. Each entry has his own peculiar technique. One gives himself a workout as the head of a large university. Another takes a job as czar of a conquered empire. Another spends his spare moments milking cows and complaining about the failure of his corn. Another assumes the editorship of a weekly magazine and then chucks it when the battle is joined. Another designs a south porch. Another writes a book and appears on "Information Please." And so on—each man grooming himself, readying himself; no two of them using the same kind of rub; each eager, attentive, nervous, articulate. Already the clockers are in the stands, timing the workouts.

"There is no liberal view," sighed the *Herald Tribune* as the old year died, "no really self-consistent and logical body of principle and policy." It was a doleful thought, and the old year drew a few more tortured breaths and expired.

Ever since Thanksgiving, the *Herald Tribune* has been rassling with the theme of liberalism, and there have been mornings when the struggle resembled an old-fashioned rassling match with the Devil. The *Tribune's* feeling about the independent liberal seems to be that he comes from a good family but has taken to hanging around pool halls. His instability, his shallow charm, his unpredictable movements, his dissolute companions, all have been the subject of speculation recently in the *Tribune's* pages, and the word that was finally trotted out to describe his fate was the word "bankrupt." Even the word, however, seemed vaguely to trouble the *Tribune,* which does not in theory approve of any sort of

American insolvency. Clearly, a dilemma. The *Tribune* met it boldly by explaining that the liberal's work was done, his victory complete, and that henceforth the "conventional party structure" would be happy to carry the whole load and take care of the situation without any help. Its editorial paid tribute to the deep moral mess of nineteenth-century liberalism and the classic insurgencies, and traced the course of liberal history from the Jefferson revolt right down to the year 1933, at which point the editorialist gulped, hawked, and spat out.

The *Tribune's* estimate of the independent liberal sounds to us a bit on the romantic side, a bit too full of the great tradition, not quite catching the essence of liberalism. The value of the liberal in the republic is not that he is logical but that he is inquisitive. At the moment, the liberal's desperate position and his dead life seem to us neither as desperate nor as dead as the *H.T.* has been making out. There are still a good many free men around who don't think that the liberal's work is done. (They would like to, but it isn't that easy.) The independent liberal, whether walking by his wild lone or running with a pack, is an essential ingredient in the two-party system in America—as strange and as vital as the trace elements in our soil. He gives the system its fluidity, its benign inconsistency, and (in cahoots with the major political organizations) its indisputable grace. We have never believed that the independent liberal had a priority on liberal thought, or a corner on the market; he merely lives in a semi-detached house and goes out without his rubbers. The *Tribune* itself has turned in such a good liberal performance lately in its news columns that its editorial shudders have seemed all the more strange. After all, it was the *Trib* that handed over ten columns last Sunday to William Z. Foster, who has seldom needed more than twenty-five words to hang himself in and this time did it in two flat, when he described legislative debates as "ridiculous talkfests."

The liberal holds that he is true to the republic when he is true to himself. (It may not be as cozy an attitude as it sounds.) He greets with enthusiasm the fact of the journey, as a dog greets a man's invitation to take a walk. And he acts in the dog's way too, swinging wide, racing ahead, doubling back, covering many miles of territory that the man never traverses, all in the spirit of inquiry and the zest for truth. He leaves a crazy trail, but he ranges far beyond the genteel old party he walks with and he is usually in a better position to discover a skunk. The dog often influences the course the man takes, on his long walk; for sometimes a dog runs into something in nature so arresting that not even a man can quite ignore it, and the man deviates—a clear victim of the liberal intent in his dumb companion. When the two of them get home and flop down, it is the liberal—the wide-ranging dog—who is covered with burdocks and with information of a special sort on out-of-the-way places. Often ineffective in direct political action, he is the opposite of the professional revolutionary, for, unlike the latter, he never feels he knows where the truth lies, but is full of rich memories of places he has glimpsed it in. He is, on the whole, more optimistic than the revolutionary, or even than the Republican in a good year.

The *Tribune* may be right that there is no liberal "view." But the question is whether there is still a liberal spirit. In these melancholy days of Hooper and Gallup, when it is all the vogue to belittle the thought in the individual and to glorify the thought in the crowd, one can only wonder. We think the spirit is there all right but it is taking a beating from all sides. Where *does* a liberal look these days? Mr. Truman has just suggested a forty-dollar bonus for all good taxpayers, Mr. Wallace has started calling people "ordinary" and man "common," and the *Herald Tribune* has liberalism on the mat, squeezing it in the kidneys. Your true liberal is on a spot, but it isn't the first time. Two dollars says it isn't going to be the last time. We'd make it five dollars except for all the talk of bankruptcy.

CARD OF THANKS

A spaniel's ears hang low, hang low;
They mop the sidewalk as they go.
Instead of burrs and beggar's-lice,
They pick up things not half so nice.

Spaniels deserve our special thanks
For mopping floors in shops and banks,
Resourceful, energetic, keen,
They keep the city nice and clean.

Spaniels should be exempt from tax
And be supplied with Johnson's wax.

—E. B. W.

LETTER TO STANLEY HART WHITE

229 East 48 Street
2 January 1949

Dear Bun:

I haven't read the book yet, as we gave a New Year's Eve party for 100 people and I'm too busy counting empty bottles and removing stains from the carpet. But I thank you and Blanche for sending me the book and hope you had a good Christmas. I am starting 1949 in a somewhat relaxed and benign condition as the result of a decision to give up the responsibility of *The New Yorker*'s editorial page.[1] I intend to apply myself to more irregular and peaceable pursuits for a while, to work patiently instead of rapidly, and to improve the nick of time. I may even try for a job on that platform which the Army hopes to establish 200,000 miles up, beyond the pull of gravity; it is conceivable that a person who no longer feels a gravitational pull might find himself no longer obedient to the pull of conscience and the pull of nationality—which would be a great joke on the Army, having gone to such trouble.

Joe returns by train to Ithaca tonight after his holidays. He likes Cornell much better than he liked Exeter. He likes soccer better than history, and he likes naval architecture better than soccer. He has a Zippo cigarette lighter, and when he pulls at a cigarette he looks to be tasting life to the very lees. His sweater is white, with red numerals 1952. Last week he registered for the draft and acquired an entirely different number.

My old dog Fred, whom you probably remember, died on Dec. 31 at the age of thirteen years and four months. With the exception of a brief spell during puppyhood when he suffered from an inflammation of the bowels, I think he never missed a meal in all those years, something of a record. Actually, he managed even to double his own record, because of a system he worked out for getting the cat's meal, too. It was a complicated system, involving accurate timing and the mastery of certain doors and stairs. In his later years, suffering from hard arteries, it cost him a lot of pain, but he never completely abandoned it.
Happy New Year to all,
En

1 Although he liked to write "Comment" and found the short paragraph a congenial form of expression, White didn't like the responsibility of producing the first page of *The New Yorker* week after week. The magazine paid him well to do it, but he found it a strain. For the second time in his life, he decided to quit the job. He continued, however, to contribute to the page.

Letter to Katharine S. White

[New York]
[Early May 1949]
Sunday aft

Dearest K:

Min and I are holding the fort this afternoon, with La Jenkins out sporting. The awful hot spell broke last night and today is clear and beautiful, with a new bird in the Garden, let us call it a Willow Pitkin. Across the street, the entire janitorial family has blossomed out in pink carnations, which Agnes says is for Mother's Day and is a sign that the Mother is alive (for those who have "passed on" the carnation is always white). Ergo: the Mother is alive, but has been "put away somewhere, in an institution." I am glad to have these matters resolved for me.

Have been having quite a bout of work since you left, and am a third of the way through my final draft of The Piece ["The Morning of the Day They Did It"]. Have reached the stage where I am suspicious that it is perhaps the lousiest concoction I have dreamed up to date, but am going doggedly ahead and will let others decide. Visited the Planetarium on Friday night (my first visit) to bone up on Space, and bought a book there on rockets. It is most helpful. . . .

Found a note in my typewriter (from Ross) on Friday, simply saying: "Ginger Rogers is in town." But have not acted. Minnie peed on the dining room rug from drinking excessive amounts of water due to the heat. I applied Dogtex and the stain is not noticeable. Have heard nothing from Joe, nothing from Atkin,[1] nothing, in fact, from anybody. . . .

There is no news of any consequence and I am writing this mostly to send my love. I have tickets to take you to see the Gi'nts play baseball next Sunday afternoon, a week from this day. I can't tell you who their opponents will be, as I am not well informed along those lines. An office boy is selecting our site in the stands and is taking the assignment very seriously. I believe he rather leans toward first base. Terry told me she always sat between first and second. That I'd like to see.

Love to all the Newberrys and to Aunt Crull, and to YOU

Andy

1 William Atkin, naval architect, who was drawing plans for a cruising boat for White. (The boat never got built.)

The New Yorker, September 3, 1949
The Talk of the Town
Notes and Comment

ARCHITECTS AND DACHSHUNDS

Serious consideration should be given by architects to the problems of people who own dachshunds. The modern boys—the Wrights, the Gropiuses, the Neutras—are full of startling ideas about functional design, but it is one thing to design a house around a person and it is something else again to design a house around a dachshund. Chief of the problems is the matter of stairs. Here, proportion is everything. An English setter takes a flight of stairs in his stride—literally in his stride, one paw after another. He merely crouches slightly and glides up or down. A dachshund, because of his low center of gravity (which in some individuals is simply a center of frivolity), is incapable of going up and down stairs one paw after another. He, or she, must tackle stairs in a series of bold, sometimes hysterical leaps, the two forepaws and the two hindpaws operating in pairs. The ascent of a dachshund is a sort of conniption. It requires considerable driving power, most of it supplied by the hind legs. The descent, far more difficult and in some instances disastrous, is a series of suicidal leaps, with the dog in imminent danger of nosing over. If you have never studied the descent of a dachshund, perhaps a brief description will help. The animal first gets himself into the correct launching position, forepaws down one step, hindpaws poised at brink of takeoff. If he is an elderly dog, he remains in the launching position for several minutes, reviewing the situation and making side remarks. Having determined to go, he throws himself outward with just enough force to drop him onto the next step down, still in the launching position. Obviously he must neither overshoot nor undershoot. And he must re-launch himself the very instant he makes contact; that is, he must continue to bounce, legs tensed and in pairs, one step at a time, till he reaches the bottom. A dachshund with long toenails descending an uncarpeted staircase makes a sound unlike any other sound in nature.

We can say with assurance that a stairway having ten-inch treads and seven-and-a-half-inch risers is a practical stairway for an adult dachshund in reasonably good health. A stairway with narrow treads—seven or eight inches, a size common in old New England houses—can cause a dachshund to crack up nervously. Circular stairs, popular with modern architects, are unfair to dachshunds; such stairs often have no risers at all, which is unnerving, and the descent requires not only a bounce but a bounce with a twist. Our own residence, built before either architects or dachshunds were highly thought of, is unsuitable for dachshunds, and we are thinking of installing an electric chair-lift for our animal. While we are at it, the chair might as well be big enough to hold both of us.

The New Yorker, December 24, 1949
(Also in *The Second Tree from the Corner* and *Notes on Our Times*)

The Distant Music of the Hounds

To perceive Christmas through its wrapping becomes more difficult with every year. There was a little device we noticed in one of the sporting-goods stores—a trumpet that hunters hold to their ears so that they can hear the distant music of the hounds. Something of the sort is needed now to hear the incredibly distant sound of Christmas in these times, through the dark, material woods that surround it. "Silent Night," canned and distributed in thundering repetition in the department stores, has become one of the greatest of all noisemakers, almost like the rattles and whistles of Election Night. We rode down on an escalator the other morning through the silent-nighting of the loudspeakers, and the man just in front of us was singing, "I'm gonna wash this store right outa my hair, I'm gonna wash this store. . . ."

The miracle of Christmas is that, like the distant and very musical voice of the hound, it penetrates finally and becomes heard in the heart—over so many years, through so many cheap curtain-raisers. It is not destroyed even by all the arts and craftiness of the destroyers, having an essential simplicity that is everlasting and triumphant, at the end of confusion. We once went out at night with coon-hunters and we were aware that it was not so much the promise of the kill that took the men away from their warm homes and sent them through the cold shadowy woods, was something more human, more mystical—something even simpler. It was the night, and the excitement of the note of the hound, first heard, then not heard. It was the natural world, seen at its best and most haunting, unlit except by stars, impenetrable except to the knowing and the sympathetic.

Christmas in this year of crisis must compete as never before with the dazzling complexity of man, whose tangential desires and ingenuities have created a world that gives any simple thing the look of obsolescence—as though there were something inherently foolish in what is simple, or natural. The human brain is about to turn certain functions over to an efficient substitute, and we hear of a robot that is now capable of handling the tedious details of psychoanalysis, so that the patient no longer need confide in a living doctor but can take his problems to a machine, which sifts everything and whose "brain" has selective power and the power of imagination. One thing leads to another. The machine that is imaginative will, we don't doubt, be heir to the ills of the imagination; one can already predict that the machine itself may become sick emotionally, from strain and tension, and be compelled at last to consult a medical man, whether of flesh or of steel. We have tended to assume that the machine and the human brain are in conflict. Now the fear is that they are indistinguishable. Man not only is notably busy himself but insists that the other animals follow his example. A new bee has been bred artificially, busier than the old bee.

So this day and this century proceed toward the absolutes of convenience, of complexity, and of speed, only occasionally holding up the little trumpet (as at Christmas time) to be reminded of the simplicities, and to hear the distant music of the hound. Man's inventions, directed always onward and upward, have an odd way of leading back to man himself, as a rabbit track in snow leads eventually to the rabbit. It is one of his more endearing qualities that man should think his tracks lead outward, toward something else, instead of back around the hill to where he has already been; and it is one of his persistent ambitions to leave earth entirely and travel by rocket into space, beyond the pull of gravity, and perhaps try another planet, as a pleasant change. He knows that the atomic age is capable of delivering a new package of energy; what he doesn't know is whether it will prove to be a blessing. This week, many will be reminded that no explosion of atoms generates so hopeful a light as the reflection of a star, seen appreciatively in a pasture pond. It is there we perceive Christmas—and the sheep quiet, and the world waiting.

Letter to H. K. Rigg

[June? 1950], Wednesday

Dear Bun:

Good to hear from you and am enclosing the description of a dachshund descending the stairs. Also a photograph that somebody sent me, to illustrate. Would like the picture back, eventually.[1] My advice, if you have a dachshund puppy, is to subscribe to the *New York Times,* and instead of reading it just distribute it liberally all over the house. In my opinion it is impossible to housebreak a puppy three months old. When they get so they lift their leg, they begin to like the great outdoors. Up until then, it's largely wasted effort. Fred, who died last year at the age of 13, was so tough and lascivious that I never hesitated to beat the tar out of him for his crimes of one sort and another. Minnie, who is now pushing eleven, is so sensitive and considerate that I don't dare speak a hard word to her, for fear it will bring on a spell of diarrhea. You have to watch out about dachshunds—some of them are as delicately balanced as a watch. . . .

Best regards,

Andy

P.S. That business about stairs is no joke. We have a flight of rather steep back stairs in Maine, and Fred nosed over twice. After that he refused the stairs, and always went around and used the front stairs (which were much flatter) even when he was in a hell of a hurry.

1 White liked the photograph mentioned in this letter so much that he later made a sketch and used it as a Christmas card in 1950.

When you come down on Christmas morn
Propelled by gravity and mirth,
We hope you find a world reborn,
Smelling of fir...and peace on earth.

KATHARINE and ANDY WHITE

Letter to Lewis Reynolds

[New York]
April 24, 1951

Dear Mr. Reynolds:

I'm very grateful for your note of condolence. Fred has been gone more than two years, but I can't see that he has slipped any. He's on my mind a good deal, and I'm not entirely sure that all his bills are paid—he charged everything.

Sincerely,

E. B. White

The New Yorker, April 21, 1951
(Also in *Second Tree from the Corner* and *Poems & Sketches of E. B. White*)

Two Letters, Both Open

New York, N.Y.
12 April 1951
The American Society for the Prevention of Cruelty to Animals
York Avenue and East 92nd Street
New York 28, N.Y.

Dear Sirs:

I have your letter, undated, saying that I am harboring an unlicensed dog in violation of the law. If by "harboring" you mean getting up two or three times every night to pull Minnie's blanket up over her, I am harboring a dog all right. The blanket keeps slipping off. I suppose you are wondering by now why I don't get her a sweater instead. That's a joke on you. She has a knitted sweater, but she doesn't like to wear it for sleeping; her legs are so short they work out of a sweater and her toenails get caught in the mesh, and this disturbs her rest. If Minnie doesn't get her rest, she feels it right away. I do myself, and of course with this night duty of mine, the way the blanket slips and all, I haven't had any real rest in years. Minnie is twelve.

In spite of what your inspector reported, she has a license. She is licensed in the State of Maine as an unspayed bitch, or what is more commonly called an "unspaded" bitch. She wears her metal license tag but I must say I don't particularly care for it, as it is in the shape of a hydrant, which seems to me a feeble gag, besides being pointless in the case of a female. It is hard to believe that any state in the Union would circulate a gag like that and make people pay money for it, but Maine is always thinking of something. Maine puts up roadside crosses along the highways to mark the spots where people have lost their lives in motor accidents, so the highways are beginning to take on the appearance of a cemetery, and motoring in Maine has become a solemn experience, when one thinks mostly about death. I was driving along a road near Kittery the other day thinking about death and all of a sudden I heard the spring peepers. That changed me right away and I suddenly thought about life. It was the nicest feeling.

You asked about Minnie's name, sex, breed, and phone number. She doesn't answer the phone. She is a dachshund and can't reach it, but she wouldn't answer it even if she could, as she has no interest in outside calls. I did have a dachshund once, a male, who was interested in the telephone, and who got a great many calls, but Fred was an exceptional dog (his name was Fred) and I can't think of anything offhand that he wasn't interested in. The telephone was only one of a thousand things. He loved life—that is, he loved life if by "life" you mean "trouble," and of course the phone is almost synonymous with trouble. Minnie loves life, too, but her idea of life is a warm bed, preferably with an electric pad,

Minnie being interviewed in E. B. White's New York office

and a friend in bed with her, and plenty of shut-eye, night and day. She's almost twelve. I guess I've already mentioned that. I got her from Dr. Clarence Little in 1939. He was using dachshunds in his cancer-research experiments (that was before Winchell was running the thing) and he had a couple of extra puppies, so I wheedled Minnie out of him. She later had puppies by her own father, at Dr. Little's request. What do you think about that for a scandal? I know what Fred thought about it. He was some put out.

Sincerely yours,

E. B. White

New York, N.Y.
12 April 1951
Collector of Internal Revenue, Divisional Office
Bangor, Maine

Dear Sir:

I have your notice about a payment of two hundred and some-odd dollars that you say is owing on my 1948 income tax. You say a warrant has been issued for the seizure and sale of my place in Maine, but I don't know as you realize how awkward that would be right at this time, because in the same mail I also received a notice from the Society for the Prevention of Cruelty to Animals here in New York taking me to task for harboring an unlicensed dog in my apartment, and I have written them saying that Minnie is licensed in Maine, but if you seize and sell my place, it is going to make me look pretty silly with the Society, isn't it? Why would I license a dog in Maine, they will say, if I don't live there? I think it is a fair question. I have written the Society, but purposely did not mention the warrant of seizure and sale. I didn't want to mix them up, and it might have sounded like just some sort of cock and bull story. I have always paid my taxes promptly, and the Society would think I was kidding, or something.

Anyway, the way the situation shapes up is this: I am being accused in New York State of dodging my dog tax, and accused in Maine of being behind in my federal tax, and I believe I'm going to have to rearrange my life somehow or other so that everything can be brought together, all in one state, maybe Delaware or some state like that, as it is too confusing for everybody this way. Minnie, who is very sensitive to my moods, knows there is something wrong and that I feel terrible, And now she feels terrible. The other day it was the funniest thing, I was packing a suitcase for a trip home to Maine, and the suitcase was lying open on the floor and when I wasn't looking she went and got in and lay down. Don't you think that was cute?

If you seize the place, there are a couple of things I ought to explain. At the head of the kitchen stairs you will find an awfully queer boxlike thing. I don't want you to get a false idea about it, as it looks like a coffin, only it has a partition inside, and two small doors on one side. I don't suppose there is another box like it in the entire world. I built it myself. I made it many years ago as a dormitory for two snug-haired dachshunds, both of whom suffered from night chill. Night chill is the most prevalent dachshund disorder, if you have never had one. Both these dogs, as a matter of fact, had rheumatoid tendencies, as well as a great many other tendencies, specially Fred. He's dead, damn it. I would feel a lot better this morning if I could just see Fred's face, as he would know instantly that I was in trouble with the authorities and would be all over the place, hamming it up. He was something.

About the tax money, it was an oversight, or mixup. Your notice says that the "first notice" was sent last summer. I think that is correct, but when it arrived I didn't know what it meant as I am no mind reader. It was cryptic. So I sent it to a lawyer, fool-fashion, and asked him if he knew what it meant. I asked him if it was a tax bill and shouldn't I pay it, and he wrote back and said, No, no, no, no, it isn't a tax bill. He advised me to wait till I got a bill, and then pay it. Well, that was all right, but I was building a small henhouse at the time, and when I get building something with my own hands I lose all sense of time and place. I don't even show up for meals. Give me some tools and some second-handed lumber and I get completely absorbed in what I am doing. The first thing I knew, the summer was gone, and the fall was gone, and it was winter. The lawyer must have been building something, too, because I never heard another word from him.

To make a long story short, I am sorry about this nonpayment, but you've got to see the whole picture to understand it, got to see my side of it. Of course I will forward the money if you haven't seized and sold the place in the meantime. If you have, there are a couple of other things on my mind. In the barn, at the far end of the tieups, there is a goose sitting on eggs. She is a young goose and I hope you can manage everything so as not to disturb her until she has brought off her goslings. I'll give you one, if you want. Or would they belong to the federal government anyway, even though the eggs were laid before the notice was mailed? The cold frames are ready, and pretty soon you ought to transplant the young broccoli and tomato plants and my wife's petunias from the flats in the kitchen into the frames, to harden them. Fred's grave is down in the alder thicket beyond the dump. You have to go down there every once in a while and straighten the headstone, which is nothing but a couple of old bricks that came out of a chimney. Fred was restless, and his headstone is the same way—doesn't stay quiet. You have to keep at it.

I am sore about your note, which didn't seem friendly. I am a friendly taxpayer and do not think the government should take a threatening tone, at least until we have exchanged a couple of letters kicking the thing around. Then it might be all right to talk about selling the place, if I proved stubborn. I showed the lawyer your notice about the warrant of seizure and sale, and do you know what he said? He said, "Oh, that doesn't mean anything, it's just a form." What a crazy way to look at a piece of plain English. I honestly worry about lawyers. They never write plain English themselves, and when you give them a bit of plain English to read, they say, "Don't worry, it doesn't mean any-thing." They're hopeless, don't you think they are? To me a word is a word, and I wouldn't dream of writing anything like "I am going to get out a warrant to seize and sell your place" unless I meant it, and I can't believe that my government would either.

The best way to get into the house is through the woodshed, as there is an old crocus sack nailed on the bottom step and you can wipe the mud off on it. Also, when you go in through the woodshed, you land in the back kitchen right next to the cooky jar with Mrs. Freethy's cookies. Help yourself, they're wonderful.

Sincerely yours,

E. B. White

The New Yorker, December 13, 1952
The Talk of the Town
Notes and Comment

NIGHT CHILL (DACHSHUNDS)

Anyone who has ever shared an apartment with a dachshund bitch knows that as the years roll on, the problem of night chill becomes increasingly difficult and finally overshadows all else in life. About ten years ago, we began to work on this baffling problem. We constructed, over the uneasy decade, an amazing series of dog beds, or devices, designed to conserve a female dachshund's body heat and thus enable her to go through the night without disturbing us. Some of these beds were beautifully constructed things—fantasies of hopeful invention, marvelous snuggle spots. Every one failed. Our aging bitch continued to leap up at about 4 A.M. with a sharp cry, announcing that she had sniffed fresh air and wouldn't be responsible for the consequences. Last week, exhausted from years of troubled nights and sleeplessness but still plugging, we cracked the riddle and split our household atom. Our discovery dwarfs all other recent marvels of science, including the H-bomb and something the Ferro Corporation has just released called "fritted trace elements" (for your soil). Ferro boasts of having worked five years to produce fritted trace elements. Hell, we've been twice that time perfecting a dachshund's night arrangement. And now, with the answer safely inside our hat, we're sorely tempted to chuck belles-lettres and get into something *really* big—something that will revolutionize dog ownership. But we're electing to take the wraps off the thing here and now, and throw it open to the public as our contribution toward a confident, well-rested America.

The way to keep a dachshund bitch warm at night is to forget about her body heat (of which she has almost none anyway) and provide her with a homemade brooder stove such as farmers rig up in their kitchen to keep baby chicks happy. You need a larger tin can (like the ones potato chips or saltines come in), a twenty-five watt bulb, a length of light cord, and a piece of cardboard. Wire the can upright to the inside of the box in which your bitch sleeps or pretends to sleep, make a cardboard top for the can, cut a generous hole in the top to receive the cord, suspend the light in the center of the can, plug in and go to bed—you and your dog, separately. The light warms the can, the can warms the dog, morning comes gently, gently; the sun returns to warm earth, man, and dog; and you can then pull the plug. Our dachshund, who will be fourteen come spring, has been sleeping with this contraption for a week now and is in love with it. The Consolidated Edison Company is, of course, in love with it, too, but we've licked that by buying a couple of shares of Con Ed stock, so our bitch's night lamp is putting profits right back into our pocket, besides giving us these long, uninterrupted sessions in the hay. And when we hear the closing Dow-Jones averages, "Rails down, industrials down, utilities up," we just look at Minnie and grin.

LETTER TO URSULA NORDSTROM[1]

25 West 43rd Street
March 12, 1954

Dear Ursula:
The beautiful copy of "Charlotte's Web" arrived and is being much admired. I show it around as though I had bound it myself. I haven't inscribed it to myself yet, as I haven't been able to think what to write on that page that tells all about how it sold so many copies, but I am looking forward to the autographing, from me to me—a wonderfully narcissistic occasion. I'm going to do it while leaning over a pool.

Anyway, this is my most beautiful book. I shall treasure it always, treasure you always, treasure Harpers always, and try not to lay up my treasure on earth but take it with me. . . . Katharine is just over mumps, I am just over shingles, Minnie is just over tapeworm, and I have just broken the third toe of my right foot. How are you?
And thanks again.
Andy

1 Ursula Nordstrom was publisher and editor in chief of juvenile books at Harper & Row from 1940 to 1973. A leather-bound copy of *Charlotte's Web* had been presented to White when 100,000 copies of the book had been printed.

The New Yorker, April 24, 1954
The Talk of the Town
Notes and Comment

ROBBED WHILE WALKING A DACHSHUND

New York seldom lets a man down. It is, as one of its admirers often remarks, "a nice little town of eight million people." The first thing we read in the paper on our return to the city was that Rudolf Bing had been held up and robbed while walking his dachshund in Central Park. Half an hour after reading of this, we were sitting in the waiting room of the veterinary hospital, thinking about what a big help a dachshund is in a holdup, when the phone rang. The girl at the desk answered, and it was Mr. Rudolf Bing calling. (Out of eight million chances.) We couldn't make out why he called; probably the incident in the Park had proved upsetting to the dog, if not to the man. We know very well how our own bitch would act in similar circumstances: she would wait quietly while we surrendered watch and wallet to the thief, and would then suggest that we both go home and to bed.

Essays of E. B. White
A Letter from the East
Turtle Bay, February 6, 1956

BEDFELLOWS

I am lying here in my private sick bay on the east side of town between Second and Third Avenues, watching starlings from the vantage point of bed. Three Democrats are in bed with me: Harry Truman (in a stale copy of the *Times*), Adlai Stevenson (in *Harper's*), and Dean Acheson (in a book called *A Democrat Looks at*

His Party). I take Democrats to bed with me for lack of a dachshund, although as a matter of fact on occasions like this I am almost certain to be visited by the ghost of Fred, my dash-hound everlasting, dead these many years. In life, Fred always attended the sick, climbing right into bed with the patient like some lecherous old physician, and making a bad situation worse. All this dark morning I have reluctantly entertained him upon the rumpled blanket, felt his oppressive weight, and heard his fraudulent report. He was an uncomfortable bedmate when alive; death has worked little improvement—I still feel crowded, still wonder why I put up with his natural rudeness and his pretensions.

The only thing I used to find agreeable about him in bed was his smell, which for some reason was nonirritating to my nose and evocative to my mind, somewhat in the way that a sudden whiff of the cow barn or of bone meal on a lawn in springtime carries sensations of the richness of earth and of experience. Fred's aroma has not deserted him; it wafts over me now, as though I had just removed the stopper from a vial of cheap perfume. His aroma has not deserted the last collar he wore, either. I ran across this great, studded strap not long ago when I was rummaging in a cabinet. I raised it cautiously toward my nose, fearing a quill stab from his last porcupine. The collar was extremely high—had lost hardly ten percent of its potency. Fred was sold to me for a dachshund, but I was in a buying mood and would have bought the puppy if the storekeeper had said he was an Irish Wolfschmidt. He was only a few weeks old when I closed the deal, and he was in real trouble. In no time at all, his troubles cleared up and mine began. Thirteen years later he died, and by rights my troubles should have cleared up. But I can't say they have. Here I am, seven years after his death, still sharing a fever bed with him and, what is infinitely more burdensome, still feeling the compulsion to write about him. I sometimes suspect that subconsciously I'm trying to revenge myself by turning him to account, and thus recompensing myself for the time and money he cost me.

He was red and low-posted and long-bodied like a dachshund, and when you glanced casually at him he certainly gave the quick impression of being a dachshund. But if you went at him with a tape measure, and forced him onto scales, the dachshund theory collapsed. The papers that came with him were produced hurriedly and in an illicit atmosphere in a back room of the pet shop, and are most unconvincing. However, I have no reason to unsettle the Kennel Club; the fraud, if indeed it was a fraud, was ended in 1948, at the time of his death. So much of his life was given to shady practices, it is only fitting that his pedigree should have been (as I believe it was) a forgery.

I have been languishing here, looking out at the lovely branches of the plane tree in the sky above our city back yard. Only starlings and house sparrows are in view at this season, but soon other birds will show up. (Why, by the way, doesn't the *Times* publish an "Arrival of Birds" column, similar to its famous "Arrival of Buyers"?) Fred was a window gazer and bird watcher, particularly during his later years, when hardened arteries slowed him up and made it necessary for him to substitute sedentary pleasures for active sport. I think of him as he used to look on our bed in Maine—an old four-poster, too high from the floor for him to reach unassisted. Whenever the bed was occupied during the daylight hours, whether because one of us was sick or was napping, Fred would appear in the doorway and enter without knocking. On his big gray face would be a look of quiet amusement (at having caught somebody in bed during the daytime) coupled with his usual look of fake respectability. Whoever occupied the bed would reach down, seize him by the loose folds of his thick neck, and haul him painfully up. He dreaded this maneuver, and so did the occupant of the bed. There was far too much dead weight involved for anybody's comfort. But Fred was always willing to put up with being hoisted in order to gain the happy heights, as, indeed, he was willing to put up with far greater discomforts—such as a mouthful of porcupine quills—when there was some prize at the end.

Once up, he settled into his pose of bird-watching, propped luxuriously against a pillow, as close as he could get to the window, his great soft brown eyes alight with expectation and scientific knowledge. He seemed never to tire of his work. He watched steadily and managed to give the impression that he was a secret agent of the Department of Justice. Spotting a flicker or a starling on the wing, he would turn and make a quick report.

"I just saw an eagle go by," he would say. "It was carrying a baby."

This was not precisely a lie. Fred was like a child in many ways, and sought always to blow things up to proportions that satisfied his imagination and his love of adventure. He was the Cecil B. DeMille of dogs. He was also a zealot, and I have just been reminded of him by a quote from one of the Democrats sharing my bed—Acheson quoting Brandeis. "The greatest dangers to liberty," said Mr. Brandeis, " lurk in insidious encroachment by men of zeal, well-meaning but without understanding." Fred saw in every bird, every squirrel, every housefly, every rat, every skunk, every porcupine, a security risk and a present danger to his republic. He had a dossier on almost every living creature, as well as on several inanimate objects, including my son's football.

Although birds fascinated him, his real hope as he watched the big shade trees outside the window was that a red squirrel would show up. When he sighted a squirrel, Fred would straighten up from his pillow, tense his frame, and then, in a moment or two, begin to tremble. The knuckles of his big forelegs, unstable from old age, would seem to go into spasm, and he would sit there with his eyes glued on the squirrel and his front legs alternately collapsing under him and bearing his weight again.

I find it difficult to convey the peculiar character of this ignoble old vigilante, my late and sometimes lamented companion. What was there about him so different from the many other dogs I've owned that he keeps recurring and does not, in fact, seem really dead at all? My wife used to claim that Fred was deeply devoted to me, and in a certain sense he was, but his was the devotion of an opportunist. He knew that on the farm I took the overall view and travelled pluckily from one trouble spot to the next. He dearly loved this type of work. It was not his habit to tag along faithfully behind me, as a collie might, giving moral support and sometimes real support. He ran a trouble-shooting business of his own and was usually at the scene ahead of me, compounding the trouble and shooting in the air. The word "faithful" is an adjective I simply never thought of in connection with Fred. He differed from most dogs in that he tended to knock down, rather than build up, the master's ego. Once he had outgrown the capers of puppyhood, he never again caressed me or anybody else during his life. The only time he was ever discovered in an attitude that suggested affection was when I was in the driver's seat of our car and he would lay his heavy head on my right knee. This, I soon perceived, was not affection, it was nausea. Drooling always followed, and the whole thing was extremely inconvenient, because the weight of his head made me press too hard on the accelerator.

Fred devoted his life to deflating me and succeeded admirably. His attachment to our establishment, though untinged with affection, was strong nevertheless, and vibrant. It was simply that he found in our persons, in our activities, the sort of complex, disorderly society that fired his imagination and satisfied his need for tumult and his quest for truth. After he had subdued six or seven porcupines, we realized that his private war against porcupines was an expensive bore, so we took to tying him, making him fast to any tree or wheel or post or log that was at hand, to keep him from sneaking off into the woods. I think of him as always at the end of some outsize piece of rope. Fred's disgust at these confinements was great, but he improved his time, nonetheless, in a thousand small diversions. He never just lay and rested. Within the range of his tether, he continued to explore, dissect, botanize, conduct post-mortems, excavate, experiment, expropriate, savor, masticate, regurgitate. He had no contemplative life, but he held as a steady gleam the belief that under the commonplace stone and behind the unlikely piece of driftwood lay the stuff of high adventure and the opportunity to save the nation.

But to return to my other bedfellows, these quick Democrats. They are big, solid men, every one of them, and they have been busy writing and speaking, and sniffing out the truth. I did not deliberately pack my counterpane with members of a single political faith; they converged on me by the slick device of getting into print. All three turn up saying things that interest me, so I make bed space for them.

Mr. Truman, reminiscing in a recent issue of the *Times*, says the press sold out in 1948 to "the special interests," was ninety percent hostile to his candidacy, distorted facts, caused his low popularity rating at that period, and tried to prevent him from

Fred on a tether, to keep him from "subduing" porcupines

reaching the people with his message in the campaign. This bold, implausible statement engages my fancy because it is a half-truth, and all half-truths excite me. An attractive half-truth in bed with a man can disturb him as deeply as a cracker crumb. Being a second-string member of the press myself, and working, as I do, for the special interests, I tend to think there is a large dollop of pure irascibility in Mr. Truman's gloomy report. In 1948, Mr. Truman made a spirited whistle-stop trip and worked five times as hard as his rival. The "Republican-controlled press and radio" reported practically everything he said, and also gave vent to frequent horselaughs in their editorials and commentaries. Millions of studious, worried Americans heard and read what he said; then they checked it against the editorials; then they walked silently into the voting booths and returned him to office. Then they listened to Kaltenborn. Then they listened to Truman doing Kaltenborn. The criticism of the opposition in 1948 was neither a bad thing nor a destructive thing. It was healthy and (in our sort of society) necessary. Without the press, radio, and TV, President Truman couldn't have got through to the people in anything like the volume he achieved. Some of the published news was distorted, but distortion is inherent in partisan journalism, the same as it is in political rallies. I have yet to see a piece of writing, political or nonpolitical, that doesn't have a slant. All writing slants the way a writer leans, and no man is born perpendicular, although many men are born upright. The beauty of the American free press is that the slants and the twists and the distortions come from so many directions, and the special interests are so numerous, the reader must sift and sort and check and countercheck in order to find out what the score is. This he does. It is only when a press gets its twist from a single source, as in the case of government-controlled press systems, that the reader is licked.

Democrats do a lot of bellyaching about the press being preponderantly Republican, which it is. But they don't do the one thing that could correct the situation; they don't go into the publishing business. Democrats say they haven't got that kind of money, but I'm afraid they haven't got that kind of temperament or, perhaps, nerve.

Adlai Stevenson takes a view of criticism almost opposite to Harry Truman's. Writing in *Harper's*, Stevenson says, ". . . I very well know that in many minds 'criticism' has today become an ugly word. It has become almost *lèse majesté*. It conjures up pictures of insidious radicals hacking away at the very foundations of the American way of life. It suggests nonconformity and nonconformity suggests disloyalty and disloyalty suggests treason, and before we know where we are, this process has all but identified the critic with the saboteur and turned political criticism into an un-American activity instead of democracy's greatest safeguard."

The above interests me because I agree with it and everyone is fascinated by what he agrees with. Especially when he is sick in bed.

Mr. Acheson, in his passionately partisan yet temperate book, writes at some length about the loyalty-security procedures that were started under the Democrats in 1947 and have modified our lives ever since. This theme interests me because I believe, with the author, that security declines as security machinery expands. The machinery calls for a secret police. At first, this device is used solely to protect us from unsuitable servants in sensitive positions. Then it broadens rapidly and permeates nonsensitive areas, and, finally, business and industry. It is in the portfolios of the secret police that nonconformity makes the subtle change into disloyalty. A secret-police system first unsettles, then desiccates, then calcifies a free society. I think the recent loyalty investigation of the press by the Eastland subcommittee was a disquieting event. It seemed to assume for Congress the right to poke about in newspaper offices and instruct the management as to which employees were O.K. and which were not. That sort of procedure opens wonderfully attractive vistas to legislators. If it becomes an accepted practice, it will lead to great abuses. Under extreme conditions, it could destroy the free press.

The loyalty theme also relates to Fred, who presses ever more heavily against me this morning. Fred was intensely loyal to himself, as every strong individualist must be. He held unshakable convictions, like Harry Truman. He was absolutely sure that he was in possession of the truth. Because he was loyal to himself, I found his eccentricities supportable. Actually, he contributed greatly to the general health and security of the household. Nothing has been quite the same since he departed. His views were largely of a dissenting nature. Yet in tearing us apart he somehow held us together. In obstructing, he strengthened us. In criticizing, he informed. In his rich, aromatic heresy, he nourished our faith. He was also a plain damned nuisance, I must not forget that.

The matter of "faith" has been in the papers again lately. President Eisenhower (I will now move over and welcome a Republican into bed, along with my other visitors) has come out for prayer and has emphasized that most Americans are motivated (as they surely are) by religious faith. The *Herald Tribune* headed the story, "PRESIDENT SAYS PRAYER IS PART OF DEMOCRACY." The implication in such a pronouncement, emanating from the seat of government, is that religious faith is a condition, or even a precondition, of the democratic life. This is just wrong. A President should pray whenever and wherever he feels like it (most Presidents have prayed hard and long, and some of them in desperation and in agony), but I don't think a President should advertise prayer. That is a different thing. Democracy, if I understand it at all, is a society in which the unbeliever feels undisturbed and at home. If there were only half a dozen unbelievers in America, their well-being would be a test of our democracy, their tranquility would be its proof. The repeated suggestion by the present administration that religious faith is a precondition of the American way of life is disturbing to me and, I am willing to bet, to a good many other citizens. President Eisenhower spoke of the tremendous favorable mail he received in response to his inaugural prayer in 1953. What he perhaps did not realize is that the persons who felt fidgety or disquieted about the matter were not likely to write in about it, lest they appear irreverent, irreligious, unfaithful, or even un-American. I remember the prayer very well. I didn't mind it, although I have never been able to pray electronically and doubt that I ever will be. Still, I was able to perceive that the President was sincere and was doing what came naturally, and anybody who is acting in a natural way is all right by me. I believe that our political leaders should live by faith and should, by deeds and sometimes by prayer, demonstrate faith, but I doubt that they should advocate faith, if only because such advocacy renders a few people uncomfortable. The concern of a democracy is that no honest man shall feel uncomfortable, I don't care who he is, or how nutty he is.

I hope that Belief never is made to appear mandatory. One of our founders, in 1787, said, "Even the diseases of the people should be represented." Those were strange, noble words, and they have endured. They were on television yesterday. I distrust the slightest hint of a standard for political rectitude, knowing that it will open the way for persons in authority to set arbitrary standards of human behavior. Fred was an unbeliever. He worshiped no personal God, no Supreme Being. He certainly did not worship me. If he had suddenly taken to worshiping me, I think I would have felt as queer as God must have felt the other day when a minister in California, pronouncing the invocation for a meeting of Democrats, said, "We believe Adlai Stevenson to be Thy choice for President of the United States. Amen."

I respected this quirk in Fred, this inability to conform to conventional canine standards of religious feeling. And in the miniature democracy that was, and is, our household he lived undisturbed and at peace with his conscience. I hope my country will never become an uncomfortable place for the unbeliever, as it could easily become if prayer was made one of the requirements of the accredited citizen. My wife, a spiritual but not a prayerful woman, read Mr. Eisenhower's call to prayer in the *Tribune* and said something I shall never forget. "Maybe it's all right," she said. "But for the first time in my life I'm beginning to feel like an outsider in my own land."

Democracy is itself a religious faith. For some it comes close to being the only formal religion they have. And so when I see the first faint shadow of orthodoxy sweep across the sky, feel the first cold whiff of its blinding fog steal in from sea, I tremble all over, as though I had just seen an eagle go by, carrying a baby.

Anyway, it's pleasant here in bed with all these friendly Democrats and Republicans, every one of them a dedicated man, with all these magazine and newspaper clippings, with Fred, watching the starlings against the wintry sky, and the prospect of another Presidential year, with all its passions and its distortions and its dissents and its excesses and special interests. Fred died from a life of excesses, and I don't mind if I do, too. I love to read all these words—most of them sober, thoughtful words—from the steadily growing book of democracy; Acheson on security, Truman on the press, Eisenhower on faith, Stevenson on criticism, all writing away like sixty, all working to improve and save and maintain in good repair what was so marvelously constructed to begin with. This is the real thing. This is bedlam in bed. As Mr. Stevenson puts it: ". . . no civilization has ever had so haunting a sense of an ultimate order of goodness and rationality which can be known and achieved." It makes me eager to rise and meet the new day, as Fred used to rise to his, with the complete conviction that through vigilance and good works all porcupines, all cats, all skunks, all squirrels, all houseflies, all footballs, all evil birds in the sky could be successfully brought to account and the scene made safe and pleasant for the sensible individual—namely, him. However distorted was his crazy vision of the beautiful world, however perverse his scheme for establishing an order of goodness by murdering every creature that seemed to him bad, I had to hand him this: he really worked at it.

P.S. (June 1962). This piece about prayer and about Fred drew a heavy mail when it appeared—heavy for me, anyway. (I call six letters a heavy mail.) Some of the letters were from persons who felt as I did about the advocacy of prayer but who had been reluctant to say anything about it. And there were other letters from readers who complained that my delineation of Fred's character (half vigilante, half dissenter) was contradictory, or at least fuzzy. I guess there is some justification for this complaint: the thing didn't come out as clear as I would have liked, but nothing I write ever does.

In the 1960 Presidential campaign, faith and prayer took a back seat and the big question was whether the White House could be occupied by a Catholic or whether that would be just too much. Again the voters studied the *Racing Form*, the *Wall Street Journal*, the *Christian Science Monitor*; they sifted the winds that blew through the Republican-controlled press; they gazed into television's crystal ball; they went to church and asked guidance; and finally they came up with the opinion that a Catholic can be President. It was a memorable time, a photo finish, and a healthful exercise generally.

The McCarthy era, so lately dead, has been followed by the Birch Society era (eras are growing shorter and shorter in America—some of them seem to last only a few days), and again we find ourselves with a group of people that proposes to establish a standard for political rectitude, again we have vigilantes busy compiling lists and deciding who is anti-Communist and who fails in that regard. Now in 1962, conservatism is the big, new correct thing, and the term "liberal" is a term of opprobrium. In the newspaper that arrives on my breakfast table every morning, liberals are usually referred to as "so-called" liberals, the implication being that they are probably something a whole lot worse than the name "liberal" would indicate, something really shady. The Birchers, luckily, are not in as good a position to create sensational newspaper headlines as was Senator McCarthy, who, because he was chairman of a Senate committee, managed to turn page one into a gibbet, and hung a new fellow each day, with the help of a press that sometimes seemed to me unnecessarily cooperative in donating its space for the celebration of those grim rites.

Prayer broke into the news again with the Supreme Court's decision in the New York school prayer case. From the violence of the reaction you would have thought the Court was in the business of stifling America's religious life and that the country was going to the dogs. But I think the Court again heard clearly the simple theme that ennobles our Constitution: that no one shall be made to feel uncomfortable or unsafe because of nonconformity. New York State, with the best intentions in the world, created a moment of gentle orthodoxy in public school life, and here and there a child was left out in the cold, bearing the stigma of being different. It is this one child that our Constitution is concerned about—his tranquillity, his health, his safety, his conscience. What a kindly old document it is, and how brightly it shines, through interpretation after interpretation!

One day last fall I wandered down through the orchard and into the woods to pay a call at Fred's grave. The trees were bare; wild apples hung shamelessly from the grapevine that long ago took over the tree. The old dump, which is no longer used and which goes out of sight during the leafy months, lay exposed and candid—rusted pots and tin cans and sundries. The briers had lost some of their effectiveness, the air was good, and the little dingle, usually so mean and inconsiderable, seemed to have acquired stature. Fred's headstone, ordinarily in collapse, was bolt upright, and I wondered whether he had quieted down at last. I felt uneasy suddenly, as the quick do sometimes feel when in the presence of the dead, and my uneasiness went to my bladder. Instead of laying a wreath, I watered an alder and came away.

This grave is the only grave I visit with any regularity—in fact, it is the only grave I visit at all. I have relatives lying in cemeteries here and there around the country, but I do not feel any urge to return to them, and it strikes me as odd that I should return to the place where an old dog lies in a shabby bit of woodland next to a private dump. Besides being an easy trip (one for which I need make no preparation) it is a natural journey—I really go down there to see what's doing. (Fred himself used to scout the place every day when he was alive.) I do not experience grief when I am down there, nor do I pay tribute to the dead. I feel a sort of overall sadness that has nothing to do with the grave or its occupant. Often I feel extremely well in that rough cemetery, and sometimes flush a partridge. But I feel sadness at All Last Things, too, which is probably a purely selfish, or turned-in, emotion—sorrow not at my dog's death but at my own, which hasn't even occurred yet but which saddens me just to think about in such pleasant surroundings.

LETTER TO LORLYN L. THATCHER

[New York]
April 23, 1956

Dear Miss Thatcher:
I see that *The New Yorker* addressed you as "Mr." Thatcher in a recent communication. My apologies.

The interpretation of my "Letter from the East"[1] by one of your pupils is quite staggering. But you can tell her that I probably wouldn't be able to do any better myself. You can also say that there are no symbols in the piece, to my knowledge. Why does everyone search so diligently for symbols these days? It is a great vogue. Fred symbolizing "the government as a whole" is such a terrifying idea that I am still shaking all over from fright—the way he used to shake from the excitement of anticipation. I'm afraid your pupil (perhaps because my wording wasn't clear) got the idea that Fred was afraid of a red squirrel. Fred wasn't afraid of a cage of polar bears laced with rattlesnakes and studded with porcupines. The only time a wave of terror would overtake him would be when he would discover that he wasn't able to emerge backwards from situations (or holes) that he had entered frontwards. He suffered from claustrophobia at this point, and was really in fright. Twice I had to take up the floorboards of buildings under which he had pursued a skunk, because even though he had managed to kill the skunk and stink everything up, he was then too exhausted and sick to his stomach to back out the way he had come in.

Please give my regards to your pupil and suggest that some day, when she's in a relaxed mood, she read the thing again, this time without symbols. Or she might try my "Letter from the South" (April 7th issue), which has no politics in it and might give her more pleasure.

Sincerely,

E. B. White

1 Of February 18, 1956, the essay "Bedfellows."

The New Yorker, May 25, 1957
(Also in *Essays of E. B. White*)
Letter from the East

A Report in Spring

Turtle Bay, May 10

I bought a puppy last week in the outskirts of Boston and drove him to Maine in a rented Ford that looked like a sculpin. There had been talk in our family of getting a "sensible" dog this time, and my wife and I had gone over the list of sensible dogs, and had even ventured once or twice into the company of sensible dogs. A friend had a litter of Labradors, and there were other opportunities. But after a period of uncertainty and waste motion my wife suddenly exclaimed one evening, "Oh, let's just get a dachshund!" She had had a glass of wine, and I could see that the truth was coming out. Her tone was one of exasperation laced with affection. So I engaged a black male without further ado.

For the long ordeal of owning another dachshund we prepared ourselves by putting up for a night at the Boston Ritz in a room overlooking the Public Garden, where from our window we could gaze, perhaps for the last time, on a world of order and peace. I say "for the last time," because it occurred to me early in the proceedings that this was our first adoption case in which there was a strong likelihood that the dog would survive the man. It had always been the other way round. The Garden had never seemed so beautiful. We were both up early the next morning for a final look at the fresh, untroubled scene; then we checked out hastily, sped to the kennel, and claimed our prize, who is the grandson of an animal named Direct Stretch of the Walls. He turned out to be a good traveller, and except for an interruption caused by my wife's falling out of the car in Gardiner, the journey went very well. At present, I am a sojourner in the city again, but here in the green warmth of Turtle Bay I see only the countenance of spring in the country. No matter what changes take place in the world, or in me, nothing ever seems to disturb the face of spring.

The smelts are running in the brooks. We had a mess for Sunday lunch, brought to us by our son, who was fishing at two in the morning. At this season, a smelt brook is the night club of the town, and when the tide is a late one, smelting is for the young, who like small hours and late society.

No rain has fallen in several weeks. The gardens are dry, the road to the shore is dusty. The ditches, which in May are usually swollen to bursting, are no more than a summer trickle. Trout fishermen are not allowed on the streams; pond fishing from a boat is still permissible. The landscape is lovely to behold, but the hot, dry wind carries the smell of trouble. The other day we saw the smoke of a fire over in the direction of the mountain.

Mice have eaten the crowns of the Canterbury bells, my white-faced steer has warts on his neck (I'm told it's a virus, like everything else these days), and the dwarf pear has bark trouble. My puppy has no bark trouble. He arises at three, for tennis. The puppy's health, in fact, is exceptionally good. When my wife and I took him from the kennel, a week ago today, his mother kissed all three of us goodbye, and the lady who ran the establishment presented us with complete feeding instructions, which included a mineral supplement called Pervinal and some vitamin drops called Vi-syneral. But I knew that as soon as the puppy reached home and got his sea legs he would switch to the supplement *du jour*—a flake of well-rotted cow manure from my boot, a dead crocus bulb from the lawn, a shingle from the kindling box, a bloody feather from the execution block behind the barn. Time has borne me out; the puppy was not long discovering Wormwood's delicious supplements, and he now knows where every vitamin hides, under its stone, under its loose board. I even introduced him to the tonic smell of coon.

On Tuesday, in broad daylight, the coon arrived, heavy with young, to take possession of the hole in the tree, but she found another coon in possession, and there was a grim fight high in the branches. The new tenant won, or so it appeared to me, and our old coon came down the tree in defeat and hustled off into the woods to examine her wounds and make other plans for her confinement. I was sorry for her, as I am for any who are evicted from their haunts by the younger and stronger—always a sad occasion for man or beast.

The stalks of rhubarb show red, the asparagus has broken through. Peas and potatoes are in, but it is not much use putting seeds in the ground the way things are. The bittern spent a day at the pond, creeping slowly around the shores like a little round-shouldered peddler. A setting of goose eggs has arrived by parcel post from Vermont, my goose having been taken by the fox last fall. I carried the package into the barn and sat down to unpack the eggs. They came out of the box in perfect condition, each one wrapped in a page torn from the *New England Homestead*. Clustered around me on the floor, they looked as though I had been hard at it. There is no one to sit on them but me, and I have had to return to New York, so I ordered a trio of Muscovies from a man in New Hampshire, in the hope of persuading a Muscovy duck to give me a Toulouse gosling. (The theme of my life is complexity-through-joy.) In reply to my order, the duck-farm man wrote saying there would be a slight delay in the shipment of Muscovies, as he was "in the midst of a forest fire scare." I did not know from this whether he was too scared to drive to the post office with a duck or too worried to fit a duck into a crate.

By day the goldfinches dip in yellow flight, by night the frogs sing the song that never goes out of favor. We opened the lower sash of the window in the barn loft, and the swallows are already building, but mud for their nests is not so easy to come by as in most springtimes. One afternoon, I found my wife kneeling at the edge of her perennial border on the north side, trying to disengage Achillea-the-Pearl from Coral Bell. "If I could afford it," she said bitterly, "I would take every damn bit of Achillea out of this border." She is a woman in comfortable circumstances, arrived at through her own hard labor, and this sudden burst of poverty, and her inability to indulge herself in a horticultural purge, startled me. I was so moved by her plight and her unhappiness that I went to the barn and returned with an edger, and we spent a fine, peaceable hour in the pretty twilight, rapping Achillea over the knuckles and saving Coral Bell.

One never knows what images one is going to hold in memory, returning to the city after a brief orgy in the country. I find this morning that what I most vividly and longingly recall is the sight of my grandson and his little sunburnt sister returning to their kitchen door from an excursion, with trophies of the meadow clutched in their hands—she with a couple of violets, and smiling, he serious and holding dandelions, strangling them in a responsible grip. Children hold spring so tightly in their brown fists—just as grownups, who are less sure of it, hold it in their hearts.

LETTER TO KATHARINE S. WHITE

[North Brooklin, Maine]
[June 1957]
Tuesday after lunch

Dear K:
I have time for just a quick note B. F. (before Forrest).[1] My rail journey was fine—they changed me into a room and I slept all night. But Bangor gave me a belly ache (beef in casserole at the Penobscot Exchange) and in Brewer, entering an upholstery shop

in search of slip-covers for the car, I slipped in a mudhole and darn near pulled my insides out of me. So when I arrived home, in rain and cold and wind, I collapsed in coils and am just beginning to emerge. Today is lovely, with a warm sun. August [a dachshund puppy] is thriving—slept all night in the plant room without disturbing anyone. He is big, bouncy, and very able. Another Fred, I would say, but without such a heavy charge of original sin. This morning I visited Allene and the children on their sunny doorstep, which is one of the pleasantest places in town for sitting. Martha is really something to see now, with her pony tail, her healthy color, and her vast affection and good will. Steve looks very fine in a new, close haircut. Allene was in the shirt you sent from Sarasota and appeared happy and healthy. Have not seen Joe yet but have talked with him on the phone, and they are coming to dinner soon. Some asparagus has been put in the freezer already. The house is in a welter of curtaining. Our crab apple tree has never had so many blossoms. A borrowed hen is on 12 bantam eggs in a horse stall, and I have a broody of my own, which I shall set tonight on 5 goose eggs. Yesterday there were wild ducks on the pond, swollen (the pond) by recent rains. Everything is green and enticing, but the weather has been on the cold side, and I don't think lilacs and apple blossoms are appreciably ahead of normal years—which is a break for you. Have not heard from Arthur yet, but imagine he will call tonight. Wearns due here Thursday, I am told, for a brief spell, so I guess I may see them.

Must go now, must arise and go on my many errands. I plan to start for New York in the car on Friday, arriving Saturday.
Love,
A

1 For many years Forrest Allen delivered the mail.

The New Yorker, October 26, 1957
The Talk of the Town
Notes and Comment

DOGS IN SPACE

The Russians, we understand, are planning to send a dog into outer space. The reason is plain enough: The little moon is incomplete without a dog to bay at it.

The New Yorker, November 16, 1957
(Also in *Writings from* The New Yorker, *1925–1976*)

White said of Fred, "Of all the dogs whom I have served I've never known one who understood so much of what I say or held it in such deep contempt." Fred was a main character in several essays: "Bedfellows" and "Death of a Pig" (Essays of E. B. White) and "Dog Training" and "A Week in November" (One Man's Meat). Fred was a spirited individualist and White continued to admire him long after his death in 1948. The "dog in the sky" Fred and White are discussing in this piece was the first animal launched in a space capsule, the Soviets' Sputnik 2, in November 1957.

FRED ON SPACE

When the news broke about the dog in the sky, I went down into the shabby woods below my dump to see if Fred's ghost was walking. Fred is a dead dachshund of mine. He is restless in death, as he was in life, and I often encounter his ghost wandering about in the dingle where his grave is. There are a couple of wild apple trees down there, struggling among the hackmatacks to gain light. A grapevine strangles one of those trees in its strong, purple grip. The place is brambly, rank with weeds, and full of graves and the spirits of the departed. Partridges like it, and so do skunks and porcupines and red squirrels, so it is an ideal spot for Fred's ghost. I went down because I felt confused about the Russian satellite and wanted to interview Fred on the subject. He was an objectionable dog, but I learned a lot from him, and on this occasion I felt that his views on outer space would be instructive.

Fred's ghost was there, just as I suspected it might be. The ghost pretended not to notice me as I entered the woods, but that was a characteristic of Fred's—pretending not to notice one's arrival. Fred went to Hell when he died, but his shade is not touchy about it. "I regret nothing," it told me once. The ghost appeared to be smoking a cigar as I bearded him for the inter-

August (Augie) at K. S. White's feet, begging for a macadamia nut

view. The interview follows, as near as I can recapture it from memory:

Q—The Soviet Union, as you probably know, Fred, has launched a second rocket into space. This one contains a female dog. Would you care to comment on this event?

A—Yes. They put the wrong dog in it.

Q—How do you mean?

A—If they wanted to get rid of a dog the hard way, they should have used that thing you have up at the house these days—that black puppy you call Augie. There's the dog for outer space.

Q—Why?

A—Because he's a lightweight. Perfect for floating through space, vomiting as he goes.

Q—Vomiting? You think, then, that nausea sets in when the pull of gravity ceases?

(Fred's lips curled back, revealing a trace of wispy foam. He seemed to be smiling his old knowing smile.)

A—Certainly it does. Can you imagine the conditions inside that capsule? What a contribution to make to the firmament!

Q—As an ex-dog, how do you feel about space in general? Do you think Man will emancipate himself by his experiments with rockets?

A—If you ask me, space has backfired already.

Q—Backfired?

A—Sure. Men think they need more space, so what happens? They put a dog in a strait jacket. No space at all, the poor bitch. I got more space in Hell than this Russian pooch, who is also sick at her stomach. Hell is quite roomy; I like that about it.

Q—The Russian dog is said to be travelling at seventeen thousand eight hundred and forty miles an hour. Do you care to comment on that?

A—Remember the day I found that woodchuck down by the boathouse? Seventeen thousand miles an hour! Don't make me laugh. I was doing a good eighteen if I was moving at all, and I wasn't orbiting, either. Who wants to orbit? You go around the earth once, you've had it.

Q—News accounts from Moscow this morning say the space dog is behaving quietly and happily. Do you believe it?

A—Of course not. There's a contradiction in terms right there. If the bitch was happy, she wouldn't be quiet, she'd be carrying on. The Russians are a bunch of soberpusses; they don't know what clowning means. They ring a bell when it's time for a dog to eat. You never had to ring a bell for me, Buster.

(This was quite true. But I felt that I would learn nothing if Fred's ghost started reminiscing, and I tried hard to keep the interview on the track.)

Q—The Russians picked a laika to occupy the space capsule. Do you think a dachshund would have been a wiser choice?

A—Certainly. But a dachshund has better things to do. When a car drives in the yard, there are four wheels, all of them crying to be smelled. The secrets I used to unlock in the old days when that fish truck drove in! Brother! If a dog is going to unlock any secrets, don't send him into space, let him smell what's going on right at home.

Q—The fame of the Russian dog is based on the fact that it has travelled farther from the earth than any other living creature. Do you feel that this is a good reason for eminence?

A—I don't know about fame. But the way things are shaping up on earth, the farther away anybody can get from it these days, the better.

Q—Dog lovers all over the world are deeply concerned about the use of a dog in space experiments. What is your reaction?

A—Dog lovers are the silliest group of people to be found anywhere. They're even crazier than physicists. You should hear the sessions we have in Hell on the subject of dog lovers! If they ever put a man in one of those capsules for a ride out yonder, I hope it's a dog lover.

(Fred's shade thinned slightly and undulated, as though he was racked with inner mirth.)

Q—This satellite with a dog aboard is a very serious thing for all of us. It may be critical. All sorts of secrets may be unlocked. Do you believe that man at last may learn the secret of the sun?

A—No chance. Men have had hundreds of thousands of years to learn the secret of the sun, which is so simple every dog knows it. A dog knows enough to go lie down in the sun when he feels lazy. Does a man lie down in the sun? No, he blasts a dog off, with instruments to find out his blood pressure. You will note, too, that a dog never makes the mistake of lying in the hot sun right after a heavy meal. A dog lies in the sun early in the day, after a light breakfast, when the muscles need massaging by the gentle heat and the spirit craves the companionship of warmth, when the flies crawl on the warm, painted surfaces and the bugs crawl, and the day settles into its solemn stride, and the little bantam hen steals away into the blackberry bushes. That is the whole secret of the sun—to receive it willingly. What more is there to unlock? I find I miss the sun: Hell's heat is rather unsettling, like air-conditioning. I should have lain around more while I was on earth.

Q—Thank you for your remarks. One more question. Do you feel that humans can adapt to space?

A—My experience with humans, unfortunately, was largely confined to my experience with you. But even that limited association taught me that humans have no capacity for adapting themselves to anything at all. Furthermore, they have no intention of adapting themselves. Human beings are motivated by a deeply rooted desire to change their environment and make it adapt to them. Men won't adapt to space, space will adapt to men—and that'll be a mess, too. If you ever get to the moon, you will unquestionably begin raising the devil with the moon. Speaking of that, I was up around the house the other evening and I see you are remodeling your back kitchen—knocking a wall out, building new counters with a harder surface, and installing a washing machine instead of those old set tubs. Still at it, eh, Buster? Well, it's been amusing seeing you again.

Q—One more question, please, Fred. The dog in the capsule has caused great apprehension all over the civilized world. Is this apprehension justified?

A—Yes. The presence anywhere at all of an inquisitive man is cause for alarm. A dog's curiosity is wholesome; it is essentially selfish and purposeful and therefore harmless. It relates to the chase or to some priceless bit of local havoc, like my experiments in your barnyard with the legs of living sheep. A man's curiosity, on the other hand, is untinged with immediate mischief; it is pure and therefore very dangerous. The excuse you men give is that you must continually add to the store of human knowledge—a store that already resembles a supermarket and is beginning to hypnotize the customers. Can you imagine a laika sending up a Russian in order to measure the heartbeat of a man? It's inconceivable. No dog would fritter away his time on earth with such tiresome tricks. A dog's curiosity leads him into pretty country and toward predictable trouble, such as a porcupine quill in the nose. Man's curiosity has led finally to outer space where rabbits are as scarce as gravity. Well, you fellows can have outer space. You may eventually get a quill in the nose from some hedgehog of your own manufacture, but I don't envy you the chase. So long, old Master! Dream your fevered dreams!

Letter to Gardner Botsford[1]

North Brooklin, Maine
6 December 1957

Dear Gardner:

The next time you are loitering at the corner of Third and 48th, looking at the girls in their winter dresses and wondering whether to drop in at the Emerald Café for a dram of Seagram's Old Hemlock, I wish you would kindly deliver a message for me to my friend Joe Vitello, who vends papers and rubs used orange juice on shoes at that intersection. I would like Joe to be told that I misinformed him about the date of the "Here Is New York" television show. He is watching for this show because he is in it, and he naturally wants to see himself in the pitchers. The correct date is Sunday afternoon, December 15. I hope you can see your way clear to deliver this simple, heartfelt message to Joe. I would drop him a line, saving you the trouble, but I have no confidence in the resourcefulness of the Postmaster General. For all I know he is at Cape Canaveral blowing on the fuse.

If this letter sounds peremptory or bossy it is because I have just dined on wild meat. My son dropped us off a haunch of venison the other day, and we pounced on it tonight, claw and fang. When our cook, Mrs. Freethy, appeared with the platter, she had a funny look on her face and before she left the room she said, "You won't give any of this deer meat to Augie, will you?" (Augie is our dachshund puppy who is bursting with the most revolting kind of health.) I replied that I hadn't planned slipping any of the venison to Augie, but why did she ask. "Well," she said, "I gave a tiny piece of deer meat to Tiny once, and Tiny almost died. She had to be rushed to the vet. It happens to dogs all the time, all over the county." Katharine and I, needless to say, settled down to our doe steak with enormous relish, and with tall overflowing glasses of replenished Scotch.

I hope you and Tassie are the same or better. Come here any time you feel like it, you will never return. And don't fail to deliver the message.

Yrs as follows,

A

1 Gardner Botsford was senior editor of the Fact Department at *The New Yorker*.

*Augie in Allen Cove, North Brooklin. When he swam,
his tail went in circles like a propeller.*

The New Yorker, September 26, 1959

(Also in *Writings from* The New Yorker, *1925–1976*)

KHRUSHCHEV AND I (A STUDY IN SIMILARITIES)

Until I happened to read a description of him in the paper recently, I never realized how much Chairman Khrushchev and I are alike. This fellow and myself, it turns out, are like as two peas. The patterns of our lives are almost indistinguishable, one from the other. I suppose the best way to illustrate this striking resemblance is to take up the points of similarity, one by one, as they appear in the news story, which I have here on my desk. Khrushchev, the story says, is a "devoted family man." Well, now! Could any phrase more perfectly describe me? Since my marriage in 1929, I have spent countless hours with my family and have performed innumerable small acts of devotion, such as shaking down the clinical thermometer and accidentally striking it against the edge of our solid porcelain washbasin. My devotion is too well known to need emphasis. In fact, the phrase that pops into people's heads when they think of me is "devoted family man." Few husbands, either in America or in the Soviet Union, have hung around the house, day in and day out, and never gone anywhere, as consistently as I have and over a longer period of time, and with more devotion. Sometimes it isn't so much devotion as it is simple curiosity—the fun of seeing what's going to happen next in a household like mine. But that's all right, too, and I wouldn't be surprised if some of the Chairman's so-called devotion was simple curiosity. Any husband who loses interest in the drama of family life, as it unfolds, isn't worth his salt.

Khrushchev, the article says, "enjoys walking in the woods with his five grandchildren." Here, I have to admit, there is a difference between us, but it is slight: I have only three grandchildren, and one of them can't walk in the woods, because he was only born on June 24 last and hasn't managed to get onto his feet yet. But he has been making some good tries, and when he does walk, the woods are what he will head for if he is anything like his brother Steven and his sister Martha and, of course, me. We all love the woods. Not even Ed Wynn loves the woods better than my grandchildren and me. We walk in them at every opportunity, stumbling along happily, tripping over windfalls, sniffing valerian, and annoying the jay. We note where the deer has lain under the wild apple, and we watch the red squirrel shucking spruce buds. The hours I have spent walking in the woods with my grandchildren have been happy ones, and I hope Nikita has had such good times in his own queer Russian way, in those strange Russian woods with all the bears. One bright cold morning last winter, I took my grandchildren into the woods through deep snow, to see the place where we were cutting firewood for our kitchen stove (I probably shouldn't tell this, because I imagine Khrushchev's wife has a modern gas or electric stove in her house, and not an old woodburner, like us Americans). But anyway, Martha fell down seventeen times, and Steven disappeared into a clump of young skunk spruces, and I had all I could do to round up the children and get them safely out of the woods, once they had become separated that way. They're young, that's the main trouble. If anything, they love the woods too well. The newspaper story says Khrushchev leads a "very busy" life. So do I. I can't quite figure out why I am so busy all the time; it seems silly and it is against my principles. But I know one thing: a man can't keep livestock and sit around all day on his tail. For example, I have just designed and built a cow trap, for taking a Hereford cow by surprise. This job alone has kept me on the go from morning till night for two weeks, as I am only fairly good at constructing things and the trap still has a few bugs in it. Before I became embroiled in building the cow trap, I was busy with two Bantam hens, one of them on ten eggs in an apple box, the other on thirteen eggs in a nail keg. This kept me occupied ("very busy") for three weeks. It was rewarding work, though, and the little hens did the lion's share of it, in the old sweet barn in the still watches of the night. And before that it was haying. And before haying it was babysitting—while my daughter-in-law was in the hospital having John. And right in the middle of everything I went to the hospital myself, where, of course, I became busier than ever. Never spent a more active nine days. I don't know how it is in Russia, but the work they cut out for you in an American hospital is almost beyond belief. One night, after an exhausting day with the barium sulphate crowd, I had to sit up till three in the morning editing a brochure that my doctor handed me—something he had written to raise money for the place. Believe me, I sank down into the covers tired *that* night. Like Khrushchev, I'm just a bundle of activity, sick or well.

Khrushchev`s wife, it says here, is a "teacher." My wife happens to be a teacher, too. She doesn't teach school, she teaches writers to remove the slight imperfections that mysteriously creep into American manuscripts, try though the writer will. She has been teaching this for thirty-four years. Laid end to end, the imperfections she has taught writers to remove from manuscripts would reach from Minsk to Coon Rapids. I am well aware that in Russia manuscripts do not have imperfections, but they do in this country, and we just have to make the best of it. At any rate, both Mrs. Khrushchev and my wife are teachers, and that is the main point, showing the uncanny similarity between Khrushchev and me. Khrushchev, it turns out, has a daughter who is a "biologist." Well, for goodness' sake! I have a *step*daughter who is a biologist. She took her Ph.D. at Yale and heads the science department at the Moravian Seminary for Girls. Talk about your two peas! Incidentally, this same stepdaughter has three children, and although they are not technically my grandchildren, nevertheless they go walking in the woods with me, so that brings the woods total to five, roughly speaking, and increases the amazing similarity.

Khrushchev's son is an "engineer," it says. Guess what college my son graduated from! By now you'll think I'm pulling your leg, but it's a fact he graduated from the Massachusetts Institute of Technology. He hasn't launched a rocket yet, but he has launched many a boat, and when I last saw him he held the moon in his hand—or was it a spherical compass?

"The few hours Khrushchev can spare for rest and relaxation he usually spends with his family." There I am again. I hope when Khrushchev, seeking rest and relaxation, lies down on the couch in the bosom of his family, he doesn't find that a dog has got there first and that he is lying on the dog. That's my biggest trouble in relaxing—the damn dog. To him a couch is a finer invention than a satellite, and I tend to agree with him. Anyway, in the hours I can spare for rest, it's family life for me. Once in a great while I sneak down to the shore and mess around in boats, getting away from the family for a little while, but every man does that, I guess. Probably even Khrushchev, devoted family man that he is, goes off by himself once in a great while, to get people out of his hair.

Already you can see how remarkably alike the two of us are, but you haven't heard half of it. During vacations and on Sundays, it says, Khrushchev "goes hunting." That's where I go, too. It doesn't say what Khrushchev hunts, and I won't hazard a guess. As for me, I hunt the croquet ball in the perennial border. Sometimes I hunt the flea. I hunt the pullet egg in the raspberry patch. I hunt the rat. I hunt the hedgehog. I hunt my wife's reading glasses. (They are in the pocket of her housecoat, where any crafty hunter knows they would be.) Nimrods from away back, Khrush and I.

Khrushchev has been an "avid reader since childhood." There I am again. I have read avidly since childhood. Can't remember many of the titles, but I read the books. Not only do I read avidly, I read slowly and painfully, word by word, like a child reading. So my total of books is small compared to most people's total, probably smaller than the Chairman's total. Yet we're both avid readers.

And now listen to this: "Mr. Khrushchev is the friend of scientists, writers, and artists." That is exactly my situation, or predicament. Not all scientists, writers, and artists count me their friend, but I do feel very friendly toward Writer Frank Sullivan, Artist Mary Petty, Scientist Joseph T. Wearn, Pretty Writer Maeve Brennan, Artist Caroline Angell, Young Writer John Updike—the list is much too long to set down on paper. Being the friend of writers, artists, and scientists has its tense moments, but on the whole it has been a good life, and I have no regrets. I think probably it's more fun being a friend of writers and artists in America than in the Soviet Union, because you don't know in advance what they're up to. It's such fun wondering what they're going to say next.

Another point of similarity: Mr. Khrushchev, according to the news story, "devotes a great deal of his attention to American–Soviet relations." So do I. It's what I am doing right this minute. I am trying to use the extraordinary similarity between the Chairman and me to prove that an opportunity exists for improving relations. Once, years ago, I even wrote a book[1] about the relations between nations. I was a trifle upset at the time, and the book was rather dreamy and uninformed, but it was good-spirited and it tackled such questions as whether the moon should be represented on the Security Council, and I still think that what I said was essentially sound, although I'm not sure the timing was right. Be that as it may, I'm a devoted advocate of better relations between nations—Khrush and I both. I don't think the nations are going about it the right way, but that's another story.

"No matter how busy Khrushchev is," the article says, "he always finds time to meet Americans and converse with them frankly on contemporary world problems." In this respect, he is the spit and image of me. Take yesterday. I was busy writing and an American walked boldly into the room where I was trying to finish a piece I started more than a year ago and would have finished months ago except for interruptions of one sort and another, and what did I do? I shoved everything aside and talked to this American on contemporary world problems. It turned out he knew almost nothing about them, and I've never known much about them, God knows, except what I see with my own eyes, but we kicked it around anyway. I have never been so busy that I wouldn't meet Americans, or they me. Hell, they drive right into my driveway, stop the car, get out, and start talking about contemporary problems even though I've never laid eyes on them before. I don't have the protection Khrushchev has. My dog welcomes any American, day or night, and who am I to let a dog outdo me in simple courtesy?

Mr. Khrushchev, the story goes on, "has a thorough knowledge of agriculture and a concern for the individual worker." Gee whizz, it's me all over again. I have learned so much about agriculture that I have devised a way to water a cow (with calf at side) in the barn cellar without ever going down the stairs. I'm too old to climb down stairs carrying a twelve-quart pail of water. I tie a halter rope to the bail of the pail (I use a clove hitch) and lower the pail through a hatch in the main floor. I do this after dark, when the cow is thirsty and other people aren't around. Only one person ever caught me at it—my granddaughter. She was enchanted. Ellsworth, my cow, knows about the routine, and she and her calf rise to their feet and walk over to the pail, and she drinks, in great long, audible sips, with the light from my flashlight making a sort of spot on cow and pail. Seen from directly above, at a distance of only four or five feet, it is a lovely sight, almost like being in church—the great head and horns, the bail relaxed, the rope slack, the inquisitive little calf attracted by the religious light, wanting to know, and sniffing the edge of the pail timidly. It is, as I say, a lovely, peaceable moment for me, as well as a tribute to my knowledge of agriculture. As for the individual worker whom Khrushchev is concerned about, he is much in my mind, too. His name is Henry.[2]

Well, that about winds up the list of points of similarity. It is perhaps worth noting that Khrushchev and I are not wholly alike—we have our points of difference, too. He weighs 195, I weigh 132. He has lost more hair than I have. I have never struck the moon, even in anger. I have never jammed the air. I have never advocated peace and friendship; my hopes are pinned on law and order, the gradual extension of representative government, the eventual federation of the free, and the end of political chaos caused by the rigidity of sovereignty. I have never said I would bury America, or received a twenty-one gun salute for having said it. I feel, in fact, that America should not be buried. (I like the *Times* in the morning and the moon at night.) But these are minor differences, easily reconciled by revolution, war, death, or a change of climate. The big thing is that both Khrushchev and I like to walk in the woods with our grandchildren. I wonder if he has noticed how dark the woods have grown lately, the shadows deeper and deeper, the jay silent. I wish the woods were more the way they used to be. I wish they were the way they could be.

1 *The Wild Flag.* (Boston: Houghton, 1946).
2 Henry Allen, White's indispensable helper on the Maine farm.

The New Yorker, May 9, 1964

Was Lifted by Ears as Boy, No Harm Done

On several occasions as a boy, I was lifted by my ears, and as far as I know I suffered no damage from these experiences. I am now sixty-four years of age, in good health. I feel an obligation to report on my ear lifts to President Johnson, who is in a corner on account of the episode with the beagles. I have never lifted a beagle by its ears, but I once attempted to remove paint from the ears of a cocker-spaniel puppy by wiping the ears with a rag dipped in turpentine, and I have been in bad odor with the humane crowd ever since. The dog is dead, of natural causes.

I freely admit that I may not be the best judge in the world of whether I suffered harm from being lifted by the ears as a boy. Some think me a bit odd—if not actually odd, at least on the odd side—and it could be that this oddness has some connection with boyhood ear liftings. I really don't know—it would be hard to put your finger on anything.

I can't remember the name of the man who used to lift me by the ears, but he was a coachman, and I think his name was Michael. All the coachmen in my neighborhood were Irishmen— it was simply easier to get along with the horse if you were Irish. I lived in a district of Mount Vernon called Chester Hill, and of about twenty houses in the block probably half of them had a stable out back. A stable usually consisted of two straight stalls, a box stall, a carriage room, a carriage washstand with drain in the floor, a harness closet, a toilet for the coachman, a manure pit, and, up above, a loft for baled hay and an oatbin equipped with a chute to carry the grain to the ground floor. There was also the coachman's room upstairs, to which boys were seldom admitted. Everything smelled wonderfully ripe: the horses, the hay, the harness dressing, the axle grease, the liniment, the coachman—

everything. This was the era when the automobile hadn't quite appeared around the bend; it was there, but it was only stumbling along. The horse was the thing.

A Chester Hill boy spent a lot of his time visiting around in other boys' back yards, and he knew the coachmen well. I was well acquainted with the interiors of most of the stables on the block, even though I had never set foot, or expected to set foot, inside the houses that belonged with the stables. The best stable was Mr. Mendel's, because he was the richest. One side of his stable had outdoor cages for pet animals, just as in the zoo.

Now back to my ears. I was in the Kellys' yard one day with a friend when Michael, the coachman, said he dared me to let him lift me up by my ears. I said, oh no you don't, not me. I was a skinny little kid, not hard to get off the ground, but I was wary. The other boy became interested though, and Michael kept teasing us along. "Come on," he said. "I wouldn't be hurting ye, ye know that." After a lot of maneuvering and hacking and filling I began weakening, and I let him put his hands on me. I was scared, but I let him. He made me face away from him. He cupped his hands over my ears very hard, and as he did so I felt his pinkies hooking themselves under my jaw, and with this grip he lifted me easily off the ground. It was just a tricky grip, to fool a boy; actually, you were being lifted mostly by your jawbone, and this doesn't hurt much. In fact, they use this sort of lift in traction, for those with trouble in the cervical spine, of whom I am one.

I have told all I remember. (There were several repeat engagements when I allowed Michael to lift me; other boys did, too, but Michael was partial to me because I was a featherweight and became airborne with little effort on his part.) But I do not want to close without saying what a privilege it is to live in a country where the outcome of the Presidential election may turn on a beagle's ears. No country like this, is there? There is no record of Mr.

Nixon's ever having handled Checkers roughly, and if it should come to a showdown between President Johnson and former Vice-President Nixon in the fall, people might forget all about Mr. Johnson's having settled the threatened rail strike. So I want him to have this little piece of extra ammunition. I mean, how I was lifted up by my ears as a boy, without damage. Or much damage.

LETTER TO CAROL[1] AND ROGER ANGELL

Sarasota [Florida]
January 9 [1967]

Dear Carol and Roger:
You will have forgotten by this time, but at Christmas you sent me a pretty tie and a sad book,[2] and I love them both. I use the tie to push me over the edge when I am at my sartorial greatest, and I use the Nathan Silver book to cry into. It's such a wonderful record. It makes me feel so OLD. You know what they were doing, don't you, the year I was born—they were beginning to demolish the reservoir at 42nd and Fifth to make way for a public library to house the books that little Elwyn White would write when he got big enough to hold a pencil. I saw my first circus in Stanford White's yellow brick Madison Square Garden, holding tight my father's hand. I covered the opening of the Roxy and the Paramount for Talk, escorting a girl named Mary Osborn to the Roxy to impress her with what a fellow I was in journalism. I went off to college, a green freshman, aboard a Hoboken ferry-boat. I was gliding into middle life when they raised the great Trylon and Perisphere, to make all the other phallic symbols around town look like peanuts. The saddest picture of all to me is the one of the Rhinelander Gardens, on West 11th, the hub of the wheel of my salad days. (There's a metaphor to rassle with!)

Well, New York may be lost, but it is not forgotten, and this exciting book will help me keep it in mind. Thank you for choosing it as a gift.

This has been a strange winter, so far, for me—the winter of the wild young dogs. I shouldn't have landed here without a full-time kennelman. These two puppies[3] need about 38 acres in which to let off steam, plus a house that their owner owns free and clear. Here, all is restriction, confinement, frustration, and discipline. I feel so sorry for them in their pent-up exuberance, I tend to spend all my waking hours and a few of my so-called sleeping hours in their company. I rise early and am out early, to get in some brisk work before breakfast. This "private" park, with its clipped cedars, sorrowing doves, well-tended lawns and rose gardens, and faintly stuffy oldsters, is not exactly a paradise for a couple of pot-smoking pups who dream of trips. We are also perilously near a highway (Higel Avenue) that rivals the East River Drive for frenetic energy, so I don't dare be too casual about liberty. What I usually do, to start the day, is to put Maggie in leash, and let Jones come along free, as an outrider. He is off like a bullet, but never really separates himself from the hunt proper, and I find I can trust him to return with us, after a quick spin around the Circle. He dashes from one pissing tree to the next, and sometimes raises his leg so high he falls over. Maggie, of course, is furious and jealous. She pulls like a steer, gagging herself and emitting horrible coughs and groans. Jones has a set-piece for an enemy—a tall, dingy, rangy yellow mongrel who emerges at the same hour (7:30 A.M.) from a known driveway. He is a sort of Yellow Dog Dingo. Spotting him, Jones bristles, then starts bouncing straight up into the air, springing from all four legs, to increase his stature. He invariably faces down this yellow dog, and puts him to rout, which he dearly loves. There is another element in it, though. Secretly, Jones wants to explore this dog and hobnob with him, and two or three times this has been accomplished, with

The young mutt, Maggie, with E. B. White;
she was later adopted by the Joel White family

sparks flying in all directions. When I return from this exhausting early-morning jaunt, I put both dogs to a hitching post (any handy doorknob) and do a preliminary cleanup of the foul kennels. I have a papier mache chamber pot that I line with sawdust, and I go to work with a trowel. This restores the yards to a semblance of order, and I can go to breakfast. After breakfast, the serious kennel work begins—freshening the beds, patting the pillows, applying new cedar shavings, relandscaping the grounds where holes have been dug, raking the runs, seeding with rye grass, refilling the water pans. And then the brushing and combing and grooming, and the laying-on of hands to discover ticks.

It all takes time. But I have two wonderful puppies, and they are responding, thank God. Maggie is highly emotional and completely adorable. Jones is peppery, scrappy, canny, and semiobedient. I think I can make a dog of him yet. I have some pictures that I'll send you when I get duplicates made.

Joe's visit with his family turned out well. The weather had chilled a bit, but was bright, and I don't think (or I didn't notice) that any of the White children thought it was anything but very hot, as they swam about five times a day. (I did my swimming about a month ago, when it really was hot, and will resume in another month, when heat returns to Florida.) Anyway, it seemed much more like Christmas to have the family here, and they all seemed in good form. I am very lucky and I am grateful for my blessings. Thanks again for your gifts.

Love,
Andy

1 Roger Angell had married Carol Rogge, then a secretary in *The New Yorker*'s Fiction Department, in 1963.
2 *Lost New York,* by Nathan Silver.
3 Maggie and Jones. White writes: "Jones was a small, poorly shaped Norwich terrier, a bundle of neuroses. He had been whelped in England.

By the time he arrived in Maine he was a nervous wreck, and had to be restored to life. Maggie, a lovable little mongrel bitch, was assigned the task and did it beautifully."

LETTER TO FRANK SULLIVAN

North Brooklin, Maine
September 13, 1967

Dear Frank:

K and I loved your letter. I feel bad that my bet failed to reach you in time for the event—the mails out of here cover the first fifty miles by dog-sled, which I believe is pulled by Chihuahuas. I also feel bad that the race was not called "The Sullivan," instead of the Frank Sullivan. Would have been a better name. The trouble with the "Frank Sullivan" is that it suggests that there is more than one Sullivan in this country, which is ridiculous on the face of it. . . .

Your admission that you "can't walk more than a few blocks" makes me feel that you are not challenging yourself enough. When I discovered that I couldn't walk more than a few blocks I immediately broke into a trot—which is what the *Reader's Digest* had been telling me to do all along—and it works very well. Creates a pretty scene on the streets and brings the roses back to your cheeks. You are not running enough, for a man of your years, and very likely you are drawing too many breaths, too. That's another thing I learned from the *R. Digest*—cut breathing down to about four times a minute. I have felt a whole lot younger since I stopped breathing. It drains your strength, breathing does. Along with my philosophy of "challenge" for the elderly, I have instituted a lot of incidental nonsense around here. I acquired a seven-weeks-old mongrel puppy from an adoption home, and there is nothing that beats a puppy for keeping a man's blood coursing in his veins. I have to get out of bed much earlier, for the first feeding, and then I have to clean up the feces, that are often cleverly hidden. I also gave instructions a year ago to have a 20-foot auxiliary sloop built for my use, which was done, and this summer has found me facing the great challenge of fog, wind, and rain at sea, among these treacherous islands and ledges, and usually alone. I don't know why, at my age, I continue to sail a boat under trying conditions, unless it is that I have a secret desire to be knighted by the Queen. Call me not Ishmael, call me Sir Elwyn.[1]

Just read your opening remarks in Corey's new book[2] and enjoyed them. I haven't read the book yet—just poked about to find references to me. I have moments of hoping and dreaming that we will live to see another Golden Age, or at least Silver Age, when writers will be both gay and disciplined and when even newspapers will show an interest in the litry life. But I dream of a lot of things. Anyway, I'm glad I lived when you did, and some others I could mention. It was a privilege while it lasted. Why, it's still a privilege!

Life here continues on its accustomed nutty round, with me dipping sheep and Katharine arranging flowers. (Read her upcoming pieces on flar arrangement in the NYer!) K suffers terribly from the mysterious skin ailment that has the dermatologists baffled and that keeps her, perforce, on a high level of cortisone. She gets tense nervously from the drug, and from not being able to wear the usual female under-attire, but she manages to raise lovely flower borders and occasionally write a piece—which is more than her little husband can say. Hell it is, I just sent a droll thing to the NYTimes, for their "Topics" column.[3] Full of fun, 750 words of pure delight. K, I am sure, will write you. Meantime we send our love and best wishes for many happy (and vigorous) returns of the 22nd.

Yrs,

Andy

1 The reference is to the knighting of Francis Chichester on his return to England after sailing around the world single-handed. White's sloop *Martha* was built by Joel White at the Brooklin Boat Yard.

2 *The Time of Laughter,* by Corey Ford.

3 A piece about computers in banks. It ran in the *New York Times,* September 23, 1967.

LETTER TO MARTHA WHITE

Sarasota, Florida
January 5, 1969

It is a cold, gloomy Sunday here today, and our thoughts turn toward home. I have just removed the Christmas wreath from the front door and took a deep breath of Maine fir as I tossed it into a wheelbarrow full of Jones's dirty bedding from his sleeping box.

We loved all the gifts that came from you and your family. It is good to get things from home when you are this far away.

My New Year began with a dog fight. A few minutes before midnight on New Year's Eve, Jones informed me that we were in imminent danger from an intruder and that we had better do something about it right away. So I crawled out of bed, put on a wrapper, snapped his leash onto Jones, and we both stepped out the front door. Someone with a flashlight was in the driveway, and then I saw Mrs. Tolman's big black standard poodle on the lawn. She called him, but instead of going to her he danced across the lawn straight for us. Jones by this time was in a terrible fury and wanted to kill the poodle. The poodle accepted the challenge, and in a jiffy I was in the vortex of a whirlpool of dog flesh that seemed to consist of about six enormous black poodles and about ten tiny Norwich terriers. It was noisy and flashy, and Jones and I were lucky to escape without being bitten. I managed to scoop him up in my arms and duck indoors. But I was shook up by the engagement, and Jones was furious that he had to go to bed without a decision. French poodles are very strange when they fight— they seem to keep their cool and operate on a high intellectual plane, like Gene Tunney.

Thank you for your good letter. You didn't tell us which of the schools you visited you prefer, or haven't you made up your mind? Grandma is still suffering from the fall she took before Christmas. Her left hand isn't of much use to her, as it is in a bandage still. I love the picture you sent. We have it propped up against the photo of *Martha* [the sloop], and everyone who comes in admires it. We are looking forward to seeing Diane and Jimmy Henderson when they come South. Give my best to Steve and John.

Love,
Grandpa

LETTER TO CAROL ANGELL

N. Brook.
[Summer 1969]
Thursday

Dear Carol:
Tell Rog that I have just sent Joe a note about the mooring, and that it should be in place by August 2.

I am terribly late in thanking you for letters and gifts. (I've lost one of the letters in the great post-Shenker[1] shuffle of mail: I've been deluged, and it is really very hampering, as about 90 per cent of the letters really call for at least an acknowledgment. I've heard from the damnedest people—a man today who said he had sailed with me by night in my catboat on the Sound, circa 1924, and I had saved his life by skillfully avoiding a collision with the

Boston night boat, which bore down upon us out of the gloom.)

I have not lost the shirt, which is beautiful, and which I love, and which is at this very moment in the hands of Virginia Allen, our seamstress, who is very clever at clipping those long Brooks Brothers sleeves off to the right length. Brooks lives in a world of gorillas. Normally, my sleeve length is 33, but to Brooks 33 is just a beginning. It is a lovely shirt, and thank you so much for it. . . .

Joe and Allene and Steven and John are cruising in *Stormy*. I think they are probably in Friendship tonight for the races. Martha stayed home, with Joy Hooper presiding, to care for the animals. Martha's duck has crossed the road, laid fifteen eggs at the base of a fence post about two feet from the shoulder of the road, and is sitting, while cars whizz by so close it ruffles her feathers. I stopped in day before yesterday, when I heard about this. Nobody was home, but Maggie took me across the highway, pointed the duck, then stuck her head under the cable (guard rail) and rested her chin on the back of the sitting duck, who never stirred.

Fred Parson has been asking for you, and others whom I can't remember. Dean Rusk was a recent house guest of the Russell Wigginses. Haying is over, thank God. Jones is well and very active in the field. My boathouse has had its face lifted, and I can now work down there no matter what the weather is. Donna's baby is beginning to show. Carol Eaton's baby is beginning to show. And come to think of it, my own stomach isn't as flat as it might be.

Everything will be a whole lot better and merrier when you and Rog get here, so hurry up. And thanks again for being so good to me on my birthday.

Love,

Andy

---

1 Israel Shenker had arrived in Maine to interview White on the occasion of his seventieth birthday, for the *New York Times*.

Letter to Carol Angell

N. Brooklin

May 28 [1970]

Dear Carol:

Happy, happy Birthday! It must be awful to be forty [she was thirty] but anyway, you are stuck with it now. At 96 [he was soon to be 71], I seem to grow younger every day. Jones is feeling his age a little bit, but not much. He is going to feel it more next week when I show up here with a West Highland White Terrier puppy named Susy. I bought Susy from a woman in Southwest Harbor the other day when I was caught in a puppy-buying mood, but I did not bring her home with me—the weather was cold and she will have to live in the barn and I didn't want her first night to be a cold one. Jones is psychic and knows something is going on that will affect him one way or another, probably adversely, and he goes around wreathed in deep suspicion. He was with me in Southwest when I made the purchase, and he smelled a rat.

My next shopping expedition will be to the Rackliffe Pottery or the Rowantrees Pottery to look for a couple of plates which are to be part of your birthday present from K and me. I wish I knew more about what color you would like and what shape. If they are for appetizers, would you like a divided-up plate or a plain plate? I hope to take K with me when I go, but right now her back is so painful she can't get into a car. . . .

The weather has smoothed out and we are in the middle of a beautiful time, crab in bloom, pear in bloom, wild pear along the roadsides in bloom, lilac buds ready to burst, many birds, and blue skies with bright sun. Saturday was a nice day at the Brooklin Boat Yard for the launching of *Cachalot*, the Peter Sturtevant sloop. It was an in absentia launch, but the owner threw a party anyway, and there was a nice crowd, which included old

Susy (West Highland white terrier) and Jones (a Norwich terrier),
January 1971, North Brooklin

Artley Parson who is 110, with his wife Charlotte. . . . Allene served drinks and fish chowder. Marianne Allen, Henry's daughter, swung the champagne bottle and hit the boat on the second try. *Cachalot* is strip-planked and is as spacious below as a ballroom. . . .

Joe Berk, from Pathways of Sound, was here last week to talk about recording "Charlotte's Web." He had already got Julie Harris to read the book, unbeknownst to me, and he brought along the tape. I didn't like it and said so, and it ended up by my agreeing to read the book myself, in my famous monotone. Berk and a technician are arriving at the Blue Hill Inn next week and I will read the book in Joe's living room after swallowing a cat pill. Joe and Allene will be away, fetching Steven and Martha. Berk, apparently, is a perfectionist . . . and I am supposed to pause in the narration every time a car goes by on the highway. I don't know what we'll do about the sonic boom or the ducks.[1]

Center Harbor is going to look like Marblehead this summer—lots of boats, including *Surfing Seal*, back from the Caribbean, and *Prudence*, the new Williamson boat—a large schooner. Mooring space is so tight, I have been chivvied out of my old location to a less desirable spot closer to the end of the sewer pipe from the Faith School of Theology.

Hope you have a pleasant birthday. Lots and lots of love. See you soon.

Andy

1 The recording session did begin in Joel White's home. However, because of continual interruptions from background noise, White managed to read only about half the book the first day. On the second day, the crew moved to the secluded house of White's friend Dr. Wearn and there completed the recording.

LETTER TO MARTHA WHITE

North Brooklin, Maine
31 May 1973

Dear Martha:
I will be thinking of you on Commencement Day and wishing I could be there to see you graduate. After four years of unremitting effort at Northfield and Mount Hermon, not to mention patience and high accomplishment, you now have something to show for it. I stole that sentence out of *Charlotte's Web* but had to remodel it a bit to fit the occasion. I send this letter off, carrying my congratulations on your achievement and carrying my love. . . .

When I think of you standing right at the edge of everything, starting off for Spain, starting off for college, there is so much that

I wish for you in life—so much of goodness and happiness and luck in the search for whatever is beautiful and fulfilling in this naughty world. My wishes fly upward and outward, and if wishing will do any good, you should have no fears for the future—all will be serene and fruitful and felicitous. And all will be deserved. The wishes of a man for his only granddaughter!

Here at home, all is rainy and green and somber and sunless. Everyone is starved for a burst of sunlight. We had a small burst yesterday, after about four weeks of dark weather, and everybody felt momentarily reborn. Susy is so dirty and filthy from living in mud, she looks more and more like an old sheep in need of shearing. She plunged into the trout pond yesterday afternoon but just stirred up the bottom and came out more bedraggled than ever. I guess I shall have to get her into a bathtub for a beauty treatment. The cold I contracted almost three weeks ago is still with me and others are having the same difficulty. Last Saturday, the Alumni Banquet at the high school became a local sensation when thirty people fell ill of food poisoning. It was the potato salad, everyone says. Lilacs and apple blossoms are all ready to spring, and the roadsides are all alight with wild pear and cherry. . . .

Congratulations, my dear Martha on your four years of study at Northfield, and I do hope you have a happy day and smiling weather for your Commencement.

Much love,

Grandpa

Philip Hewes, a New Yorker *reader (who had mentioned his lapsed subscription) and a dog fancier, had picked up a copy of* One Man's Meat *while he was bedridden and had written to White to inquire whether he still owned a Norwich terrier. Hewes later passed White's reply on to the* Norwich Terrier News, *published by the Norwich Terrier Club, U.S.A., and it was printed in their Spring, 1975 issue.*

LETTER TO PHILIP HEWES

North Brooklin, Maine
March 20, 1974

Dear Mr. Hewes:
Sorry to hear that you are a dropout but am grateful for your letter and glad you can still read. Wish I could still write.

My Norwich Terrier will be seven in May. His Club name is Jaysgreen Rusty (United Kingdom), and he was sired (it says here) by a dog named Hunston Horseradish. He is known in this house as Jones and is seldom found more than six feet from where I am. He is a neurotic—scarred as a puppy by being shoved into a crate for a plane trip from England, then another plane trip from Boston to Maine. I think somebody along the way must have hit him with a stick, because even after all these years with me, I can't pick up a fly swatter without his cringing. I got him from Sylvia Warren, and he almost never made it up out of his bed of neuroses. But he and I are enough alike so that we get on well, and I can't help being touched by his loyalty—which I think in his case is simply insecurity. He would never take a prize at a show. Neither would I, come to think of it.

I have another terrier—a West Highland White, or Off White, named Susy. She is as open and outgiving as Jones is closed and reserved. Everybody loves Susy. Everybody tries to like Jones. But Jones takes his guard duties seriously and has made several attempts to kill people he thought were intruding. He particularly distrusts women in trousers, drivers of panel trucks, small children, and stray dogs. He has hunted squirrels for six years without bagging one. Susy is quicker than he is and once nabbed a barn swallow on the wing. Sometimes I dream of owning another Norwich—one that looks like a Norwich and behaves like one. But I am known for my outsize dreams. Meantime, I am grateful for small favors, like the little brown one over there on the sofa.

Sincerely,

E. B. White

LETTER TO JON[1] AND CINDY STABLEFORD

North Brooklin, Maine
April 8, 1978

Dear Jon and Cindy:

It was a week ago that you took me in and restored me to life after that long and tiring journey,[2] and I am ashamed that I have not got off a thank-you note before this. My only excuse is that I had never had such an accumulation of backed-up work to return to. My room is still a mare's nest, although I've been digging around in it for seven days. . . .

The drive home with Henry Allen was uneventful except that in midpassage I managed to break a tooth. We have two dentists in Blue Hill now: one is away on vacation, the other was called away because of sickness in his family. So I am just living with my busted tooth, which luckily does not send out any signals that amount to anything. Jones was so glad to see me back he went all around with me through the rooms, making queer little groans of pleasure, and then took up a stand outside the bathroom door and howled. One day while I was away he found a wool shirt of mine in the living room and proceeded to take it all to pieces, whether from anger or from uneasiness I do not know.

Thank you again for all you did—for putting me up at the Inn, for wining and dining me, for giving me a restful evening, and for driving me to Freeport. It was a lovely ending to a long trip. I thought the model of your Vermont house looked very promising, and I hope you will both get a lot of fun out of creating something out of nothing.

We still have snow and ice here, but my goose is laying and the snowdrops are in bloom in the bulb garden. My greenhouse looks like an advertisement for a greenhouse.

Much love,
Andy

1 Jon Stableford is the son of Katharine White's daughter, Nancy (Angell) Stableford.
2 EBW had been to Sarasota, Florida, with Roger and Carol Angell, while Roger was visiting ballparks there and writing a piece on spring training.

LETTER TO MRS. SUSAN [LOVENBURG] ROBINSON

[January 1984]
[North Brooklin, Maine]

Dear Susan:
I've owed you a letter for a long time, but I'm getting lazier and lazier about writing. I can see only one half of the keyboard with my one eye, and that slows me up in itself.

Well, the Great Scott Elledge adventure has at last come to a head, after sixteen years of his wanderings in the darkest corners of the Cornell Library. The book is out and Scott can relax at last, even if I can't. His publisher is throwing a party for him on the fif-

Red with E. B. White (in his eye patch), early 1984. (Photo by Bette Britt)

teenth at the Coffee House in New York. I shall remain quietly in Brooklin. The *New York Times Book Review* is after me for a "recent" photograph, to accompany their upcoming review[1] of the biography. I am billed on the jacket as America's "most beloved" writer, and I have already told Scott what a mistake that is, since people really want to read about someone they can loathe. The *Washington Post* noticed the book briefly a while back, pointing out that my life really hadn't been interesting enough to warrant a biography. On the other hand, I got a letter this week from John Detmold, a friend of mine who went to Cornell, and he raves about the book and says Scott should be nominated for a Pulitzer.

I am reading the book from cover to cover. A chapter a day is about all I can manage with my failed vision. I must say Scott has done an incredible amount of homework—he has dredged up all kinds of things I'd forgotten or never even knew about or wanted to forget or wanted not to know about. But I'm afraid there is just too much of everything. Scott simply became infatuated with the sound of his own research and couldn't bear to leave out anything, however trivial, however dull. I dread seeing the reviews—not on my account but on his. Still, one never knows. Maybe the book will go.

I've had a dull and sickly winter, with not much going on either inside or outside of my head. I envy you and Peter your trip to France. There's just a chance I may get to Sarasota for a while in April—Corona has a short vacation and wants to go down.

My little dog Red has turned out very well. He is a natural enthusiast and wants to know everything and go everywhere. Makes a good companion if you can stand his ebullience.

I hope life in Lelystad will continue to amuse and sustain you. Many thanks for your good letter.

Yrs,

Andy

1 The review by Russell Lynes, titled "The Divided Life of Stuart Little's Father," was published in their February 26, 1984, issue. It begins, "Near the beginning of his nice biography of E. B. (Andy) White, a very nice and very gifted man . . ." and it is what you might call a nice review. The "recent" photo shows EBW wearing his eye patch.

LETTER TO HENRY —

[ca. March 1984]
[North Brooklin, Maine]

Dear Henry:

Thanks for the bumpy ride down Memory Lane. It reached a high point when you exclaimed, "What I remember most about you is that beautiful collie, Caesar." (His name was Mac. He was a good dog, though.)

I don't want you to go around thinking that you are the only M.V.H.S. graduate who ever hears from his old high school sweetheart. I had a chatty letter from Mildred Hesse just the other day. She's the official historian of Garden City, Long Island, and has written a book about the place. I don't remember Marien Robinson, which can only mean that she wasn't as pretty as Mildred Hesse. I remember the way Frank Gaebelein could play the piano—as though he was in a hurry to get somewhere before it started to rain. There was another guy named Sheridan who could play better, but I don't think he ever went to classes. Just played the piano.

You can tell your neighbor's daughter that a coyote came out of the woods one day last spring when I was riding my old Raleigh 3-speed bicycle on the highway and loped along after me for fifty yards out of, I think, simple curiosity. It could have been his first glimpse of an octogenarian on wheels.

End of nostalgia. There's no chance of old acquaintance being forgot as long as my beautiful collie Caesar lives in memory.

Yrs,

[E.B. White]

Young Elwyn's first dog, a collie named Mac